The Blue Book of Grammar and Punctuation

An Easy-to-Use Guide
with Clear Rules, Real-World Examples,
and Reproducible Quizzes

Tenth Edition

Jane Straus

JOSSEY-BASS
A Wiley Imprint
www.josseybass.com

Published by Jossey-Bass
A Wiley Imprint
989 Market Street, San Francisco, CA 94103-1741   www.josseybass.com

Readers should be aware that Internet Web sites offered as citations and/or sources for further information may have changed or disappeared between the time this was written and when it is read.

Limit of Liability/Disclaimer of Warranty: While the publisher and author have used their best efforts in preparing this book, they make no representations or warranties with respect to the accuracy or completeness of the contents of this book and specifically disclaim any implied warranties of merchantability or fitness for a particular purpose. No warranty may be created or extended by sales representatives or written sales materials. The advice and strategies contained herein may not be suitable for your situation. You should consult with a professional where appropriate. Neither the publisher nor author shall be liable for any loss of profit or any other commercial damages, including but not limited to special, incidental, consequential, or other damages.

Jossey-Bass books and products are available through most bookstores. To contact Jossey-Bass directly call our Customer Care Department within the U.S. at 800-956-7739, outside the U.S. at 317-572-3986, or fax 317-572-4002.

Jossey-Bass also publishes its books in a variety of electronic formats. Some content that appears in print may not be available in electronic books.

ISBN: 978-0-470-22268-3

Printed in the United States of America
TENTH EDITION
PB Printing   10 9 8 7 6 5 4 3 2 1

Contents

To my wonderful husband, Lester Kaufman, who spares me from embarrassment by being the most tenacious, relentless proofreader a gal could ask for. (It's fine to end a sentence with a preposition . . . really!)

Acknowledgments

Creating and publishing a reference guide and workbook that is popular, easy to understand, and tempting to use requires the input of many. My thanks go to the following: my parents who, as immigrants to the United States, passed their meticulousness about speaking and writing well along to me; Gary Klehr for helping to name the book many years ago and for tireless structural editing; my husband, Lester Kaufman, for catching so many mistakes before they found their way into print; our daughter, Zoe, for her wise counsel about content and much more; my literary agent, Cathy Fowler, for her steadfast belief in the book's value; Marjorie McAneny at Jossey-Bass Publishers for enthusiastically rolling out the red carpet; and the thousands of loyal readers and viewers of my Web site who, by offering valuable input daily, help shape every rule, example, and quiz.

About the Author

IN 1975, when the State of California was formulating its plan for a training branch, no one knew what employees wanted or needed. **Jane Straus**, then an undergraduate at the University of California at Davis seeking work as a waitress, was offered the job of finding out in exchange for three units toward graduation. From her interviews with hundreds of State employees, Jane discovered that they needed English and math programs to pass the civil service promotional exams. She sent in her results, received her units, and kept knocking on restaurant doors. One day, she got a call: "Jane, it looks as though you can write well. Can you teach a class in English?" Desperate and too naïve to know better, Jane answered with a resounding, "Sure." This is how a star was born—or at least began to rise in the sky. Within weeks, thirty employees signed up for a one-day trial program in Basic English Grammar and Punctuation Skills taught by (twenty-year-old) "Training Consultant" Jane Straus. To prepare, Jane scoured the library for materials but found no books that conveyed the rules of English in—well—plain English. So she wrote the rules her way, made up some exercises, ran off some copies, and hoped for the best that first day of class. Fortunately, the class raved about Jane and her material, but she still searched for "real" work. What she didn't know was that the phones at the newly formed State Training Center were ringing off the hook. Word had spread quickly. More and more State employees demanded that they get an equal opportunity to benefit from Jane's seminar. Eventually, Jane taught many different courses for state and federal employees as well as for the private sector and nonprofit organizations. Some of the programs she designed included Public Speaking (where she met her wonderful husband), Effective Meeting Skills, and Communicating with Different Personality Styles. While developing these programs, she continued to refine her English material, eventually turning it into *The Blue Book of Grammar and Punctuation*.

Jane believed that this easy-to-use guide and workbook should be offered to everyone as a self-help tool. When the Internet was born, she saw a perfect opportunity to cast the net wide and offered the entire contents of *The Blue Book* online for free, as it still is today. During her tenure as a consultant, Jane also began a coaching and consulting practice to help individuals, couples, families, and organizations communicate truthfully, effectively, and compassionately. Her corporate retreats and keynote speeches have made her a sought-after speaker, and her private life-coaching practice thrives. In 2003, at the top of her game, Jane was diagnosed with a brain tumor, giving her an opportunity to assess her life (and perhaps her imminent death). Gratefully, the noncancerous tumor was successfully removed. Also gone were Jane's fears about taking her self-help work to the next level. She wrote her inspirational book, *Enough Is Enough! Stop Enduring and Start Living Your Extraordinary Life*, over the next year and it was published in 2005 by Jossey-Bass. She has become a favorite guest expert in the media and writes articles for publication. People often ask Jane how she blends her English teacher persona with her wit and wisdom in matters of the heart and spirit. Her answer is, "It's all self-help. Whether I'm figuring out a way to explain the use of a semicolon or working with someone who wants to stop suffering from addiction, resentment, or shame, there is a path. My art and skill lie in making that path look and feel like a stroll instead of a steep climb up a treacherous mountain. It's the ultimate gratification when someone I'm working with says, 'I get it. I didn't know it could be so easy.' Whether they are referring to the distinction between *who* and *whom* or they're celebrating life in new and extraordinary ways because of our work together, it's music to my ears and a gift to my spirit."

Foreword

The Blue Book of Grammar and Punctuation succeeds at a rare feat: being many things to many people. It's a refresher for experts, a reference for lay people, and a lesson plan for teachers. Now in its tenth edition, *The Blue Book* is a masterpiece of clarity and usefulness.

I first became aware of *The Blue Book* when I was working on the transcripts for my audio podcast, *Grammar Girl's Quick and Dirty Tips for Better Writing*. Much like Jane at the beginning of her career as a corporate trainer specializing in English instruction, I embarked upon my role as a usage commentator with a love of language, an optimistic outlook, and no idea what I was getting myself into.

Also like Jane, my efforts met with unexpected success, and I suddenly found myself on tight deadlines and knee deep in every manner of language book. My listeners and readers seemed to revel in their role as after-the-fact copy editors, and I needed all the help I could get. I noticed that one Web site kept coming up in my searches—Jane's Grammarbook.com. Every entry provided a clear answer to my questions, and I just had to have the book for myself.

I reach for *The Blue Book* almost every day because it covers the most common grammar and punctuation questions. I'm also excited about the tenth edition's inclusion of Confusing Words and Homonyms. For me, the book serves both as a refresher and as a quick double check on what I'm pretty sure I already know. But for businesspeople who aren't already stuffed full of English usage rules, this book is an essential reference to have on hand when writing e-mails, business letters, reports, and the like. Should you use *affect* or *effect*? A semicolon or comma? *The Blue Book* is your trusty guide.

In addition, with dozens of quizzes specifically designed for before-and-after testing, *The Blue Book* is perfect for classroom teachers and home-schoolers. An instructor can pretest students, go through a lesson, and then administer a posttest to show students how much they have learned. Even though I'm not in school, I took all the quizzes. Is there anyone who doesn't like quizzes? There's a reason practically every magazine includes them!

As it goes into its tenth edition, *The Blue Book* deserves its reputation as a true classic. Author Jane Straus has a gift for distilling the rules down to their essence and clarifying with real-world examples to create this comprehensible learning tool and reference guide. This book will help you not only feel smarter; you will *be* smarter and have fun in the process.

Gilbert, Arizona   Mignon Fogarty—Grammar Girl
June 2007   www.quickanddirtytips.com

Introduction

NOW IN ITS TENTH EDITION, *The Blue Book of Grammar and Punctuation* will help you write and speak with confidence. Contrary to what may be your past experience, you don't have to be an English major to understand grammar and punctuation. You just need rules that are easy to understand with real-world examples.

Whether you are an instructor teaching students the rules of English or a student, executive, professional writer, or avid blogger honing your grammar and punctuation skills, this book will help you zip through tests (including the SAT), reports, essays, letters, e-mails, and resumes and will make you (or at least your writing) look impressive.

This book is logical, self-paced, and fun to use, with scores of interesting and challenging quizzes that may be photocopied to your heart's content. Best of all, you can look forward to instant gratification because the answers are included.

If you don't want to interrupt your thoughts to figure out where the next comma should go or whether to write *who* or *whom*, you will find *The Blue Book* a pleasure to use. Dedicated to eliminating unnecessary jargon, it highlights the most important grammar, punctuation, and capitalization rules and clarifies the most commonly confused words.

The Blue Book begins with Chapter One, Grammar. Here, you will learn how to locate Subjects and Verbs so that you can make sure they agree with each other. Then you will move on to Pronoun Usage so that you will know whether to write *I* or *me*, *he* or *him*, *who* or *whom*, and so forth. From there, in the Adjective and Adverb chapter, you will discover why some words have *-ly* added to them and why you must say, "She did well on the test," not, "She did good on the test." After that, you will breeze through Prepositions where you will find some surprising rules and we will debunk at least one myth. *Hint:* Is it safe to ask, "What are you talking about?" or must we ask, "About what are you talking?"

The Effective Writing section of this chapter will give you helpful tips to be able to construct sentences and paragraphs that flow gracefully, making it easier to write quickly and well.

After that, you will enjoy spending time reading all about *affect* vs. *effect, lay* vs. *lie, their* vs. *there* vs. *they're,* and *its* vs. *it's* in Chapter Two, Confusing Words and Homonyms. I have provided hundreds of words for you in this chapter so you will never have to be confused between *farther* and *further, continual* and *continuous,* and all the rest of the trickiest words in the English language.

Chapter Three, Punctuation, contains all the usual suspects: Periods (including spacing suggestions), Ellipsis marks, Commas, Semicolons, Colons, Question marks, Quotation marks, Parentheses, Apostrophes, Hyphens, and Dashes. The best part about these chapters is that you will find an abundance of examples that you run across every day.

Then comes Chapter Four, Capitalization, where you will get your most vexing questions answered, such as which words to capitalize in a title, when to capitalize job titles like *president* or *director,* and if it's really true that *summer* and *fall* are lowercase.

In Chapter Five, Writing Numbers, you will learn when to use numerals and when to write out numbers as well as how to write both fractions and large numbers.

Promise not to skip the Quizzes, Pretests, or Mastery Tests in Chapter Six. The more you practice, the more confident you will become. Once you get over any fears about test taking, I think you will find the quizzes both fun and intriguing. You will find the answers in Chapter Seven.

Please visit www.Grammarbook.com, where you will find all the quizzes in the book in multiple-choice, interactive format. Plus, if you are a teacher or really jazzed about improving your English skills, on this Web site you will find:

- Hundreds of additional downloadable, interactive quizzes in the Subscription area

- All the rules and examples you see in the book

- A sign-up box on the home page for my free weekly e-newsletter with tips and articles

- My blog

- Recommendations for further reading and study

I hope you find *The Blue Book* to be both enjoyable and invaluable. To send an acknowledgment (always appreciated) or to offer feedback or suggestions, write to me at Jane@janestraus.com.

Chapter 1

Grammar

Finding Subjects and Verbs

Being able to find the right subject and verb will help you correct errors of agreement.

> **Example:** *The list of items is/are on the desk.*
>
> > If you know that *list* is the subject, then you will choose *is* for the verb.

Being able to identify the subject and verb correctly will also help you with commas and semicolons as you will see later.

Definition. A **Verb** is a word that shows action (*runs, hits, slides*) or state of being (*is, are, was, were, am,* and so on).

> **Examples:** *He ran around the block.*
> > *You are my friend.*

Rule 1. If a verb follows *to,* it is called an infinitive phrase and is not the main verb. You will find the main verb either before or after the infinitive phrase.

> **Examples:** *I like to walk.*
> > *The efforts to get her elected succeeded.*

Definition. A **Subject** is the noun or pronoun that performs the verb.

> **Example:** *The woman hurried.*
> > *Woman* is the subject.

Rule 2. A subject will come before a phrase beginning with *of*.

Example: A <u>bouquet</u> *of yellow roses* <u>will lend</u> *color and fragrance to the room.*

Rule 3. To find the subject and verb, always find the verb first. Then ask who or what performed the verb.

Examples: The jet engine passed inspection. Passed is the verb. Who or what passed? The *engine*, so *engine* is the subject. If you included the word *jet* as the subject, lightning will not strike you. Technically, *jet* is an adjective here and is part of what is known as the complete subject.
From the ceiling **hung** *the chandelier.* The verb is *hung.* Now, if you think *ceiling* is the subject, slow down. Ask *who* or *what* hung. The answer is *chandelier*, not *ceiling.* Therefore, *chandelier* is the subject.

Rule 4. Any request or command such as "Stop!" or "Walk quickly." has the understood subject *you* because if we ask who is to stop or walk quickly, the answer must be *you.*

Example: (<u>You</u>*) Please* <u>bring</u> *me some coffee.*
Bring is the verb. Who is to do the bringing? *You* understood.

Rule 5. Sentences often have more than one subject, more than one verb, or pairs of subjects and verbs.

Examples: <u>I</u> <u>like</u> *cake and* <u>he</u> <u>likes</u> *ice cream.*
Two pairs of subjects and verbs
<u>He</u> *and* <u>I</u> <u>like</u> *cake.*
Two subjects and one verb
<u>She</u> <u>lifts</u> *weights and* <u>jogs</u> *daily.*
One subject and two verbs

Subject and Verb Agreement

Basic Rule. The basic rule states that a singular subject takes a singular verb, while a plural subject takes a plural verb.

Note

The trick is in knowing whether the subject is singular or plural. The next trick is recognizing a singular or plural verb.

Hint: Verbs do not form their plurals by adding an *s* as nouns do. In order to determine which verb is singular and which one is plural, think of which verb you would use with *he* or *she* and which verb you would use with *they.*

> *Example: talks, talk*
>> Which one is the singular form? Which word would you use with *he*? We say, "He talks." Therefore, *talks* is singular. We say, "They talk." Therefore, *talk* is plural.

Rule 1. Two singular subjects connected by *or* or *nor* require a singular verb.

> *Example: My <u>aunt</u> or my <u>uncle</u> <u>is arriving</u> by train today.*

Rule 2. Two singular subjects connected by *either/or* or *neither/nor* require a singular verb as in Rule 1.

> *Examples: Neither Juan nor Carmen is available.*
>> *Either <u>Kiana</u> or <u>Casey</u> <u>is helping</u> today with stage decorations.*

Rule 3. When *I* is one of the two subjects connected by *either/or* or *neither/nor*, put it second and follow it with the singular verb *am.*

> *Example: Neither <u>she</u> nor <u>I</u> <u>am going</u> to the festival.*

Rule 4. When a singular subject is connected by *or* or *nor* to a plural subject, put the plural subject last and use a plural verb.

> *Example: The <u>serving bowl</u> or the <u>plates</u> <u>go</u> on that shelf.*

Rule 5. When a singular and plural subject are connected by *either/or* or *neither/nor*, put the plural subject last and use a plural verb.

> *Example: Neither <u>Jenny</u> nor the <u>others</u> <u>are</u> available.*

Rule 6. As a general rule, use a plural verb with two or more subjects when they are connected by *and.*

> *Example: A <u>car</u> and a <u>bike</u> <u>are</u> my means of transportation.*

Rule 7. Sometimes the subject is separated from the verb by words such as *along with, as well as, besides,* or *not.* Ignore these expressions when determining whether to use a singular or plural verb.

Examples: *The <u>politician</u>, along with the newsmen, <u>is expected</u> shortly.*
Excitement, as well as nervousness, <u>is</u> the cause of her shaking .

<u>**Rule 8.**</u> The pronouns *each, everyone, every one, everybody, anyone, anybody, someone,* and *somebody* are singular and require singular verbs. Do not be misled by what follows *of*.

Examples: *<u>Each</u> of the girls <u>sings</u> well.*
Every <u>one</u> of the cakes <u>is</u> gone.

Note

Everyone is one word when it means *everybody*. *Every one* is two words when the meaning is *each one*.

<u>**Rule 9.**</u> With words that indicate portions—*percent, fraction, part, majority, some, all, none, remainder,* and so forth—look at the noun in your *of* phrase (object of the preposition) to determine whether to use a singular or plural verb. If the object of the preposition is singular, use a singular verb. If the object of the preposition is plural, use a plural verb.

Examples: *<u>Fifty percent</u> of the pie <u>has</u> disappeared.*
Pie is the object of the preposition *of*.
<u>Fifty percent</u> of the pies <u>have</u> disappeared.
Pies is the object of the preposition.
<u>One-third</u> of the city <u>is</u> unemployed.
<u>One-third</u> of the people <u>are</u> unemployed.

Note

Hyphenate all spelled-out fractions.

<u>All</u> of the pie <u>is</u> gone.
<u>All</u> of the pies <u>are</u> gone.

<u>Some</u> of the pie <u>is missing</u>.
<u>Some</u> of the pies <u>are missing</u>.

<u>None</u> of the garbage <u>was picked</u> up.
<u>None</u> of the sentences <u>were punctuated</u> correctly.
Of all her books, <u>none</u> <u>have sold</u> as well as the first one.

Note

Apparently, the SAT testing service considers *none* as a singular word only. However, according to *Merriam Webster's Dictionary of English Usage,* "Clearly *none* has been both singular and plural since Old English and still is. The notion that it is singular only is a myth of unknown origin that appears to have arisen in the 19th century. If in context it seems like a singular to you, use a singular verb; if it seems like a plural, use a plural verb. Both are acceptable beyond serious criticism" (p. 664). When *none* is clearly intended to mean *not one* or *not any,* it is followed by a singular verb.

Rule 10. When *either* and *neither* are subjects, they always take singular verbs.

> *Examples: Neither of them is available to speak right now.*
> *Either of us is capable of doing the job.*

Rule 11. The words *here* and *there* have generally been labeled as adverbs even though they indicate place. In sentences beginning with *here* or *there,* the true subject follows the verb.

> *Examples: There are four hurdles to jump.*
> *There is a high hurdle to jump.*

Rule 12. Use a singular verb with sums of money or periods of time.

> *Examples: Ten dollars is a high price to pay.*
> *Five years is the maximum sentence for that offense.*

Rule 13. Sometimes the pronoun *who, that,* or *which* is the subject of a verb in the middle of the sentence. The pronouns *who, that,* and *which* become singular or plural according to the noun directly in front of them. So, if that noun is singular, use a singular verb. If it is plural, use a plural verb.

> *Examples: Salma is the scientist who writes/write the reports.*
> The word in front of *who* is *scientist,* which is singular.
> Therefore, use the singular verb *writes.*
> *He is one of the men who does/do the work.*
> The word in front of *who* is *men,* which is plural.
> Therefore, use the plural verb *do.*

Rule 14. Collective nouns such as *team* and *staff* may be either singular or plural depending on their use in the sentence.

> *Examples: The staff is in a meeting.*
> *Staff* is acting as a unit here.
> *The staff are in disagreement about the findings.*

The staff are acting as separate individuals in this example. The sentence would read even better as:
The staff members are in disagreement about the findings.

Pronouns

Definition. A **pronoun** is a word that takes the place of a noun. Pronouns can be in one of three cases: Subject, Object, or Possessive.

Rule 1. Subject pronouns are used when the pronoun is the subject of the sentence. You can remember subject pronouns easily by filling in the blank subject space for a simple sentence.

>   *Example:* _____ *did the job.*
>
>   > *I, you, he, she, it, we,* and *they* all fit into the blank and are, therefore, subject pronouns.

Rule 2. Subject pronouns are also used if they rename the subject. They will follow *to be* verbs such as *is, are, was, were, am,* and *will be.*

>   *Examples: It is he.*
>
>   > *This is she speaking.*
>   >
>   > *It is we who are responsible for the decision to downsize.*

Note

In spoken English, most people tend to follow *to be* verbs with Object pronouns. Many English teachers support (or at least have given in to) this distinction between written and spoken English.

>   *Example: It could have been them.*
>   **Better:**   *It could have been they.*
>   *Example: It is just me at the door.*
>   **Better:**   *It is just I at the door.*

Rule 3. Object pronouns are used everywhere else (direct object, indirect object, object of the preposition). Object pronouns are *me, you, him, her, it, us,* and *them.*

>   *Examples: Jean talked to him.*
>
>   > *Are you talking to me?*

To be able to choose pronouns correctly, you must learn to identify clauses. A clause is a group of words containing a verb and subject.

Rule 4a. A **strong clause** can stand on its own.

>   *Examples: She is hungry.*
>
>   > *I am feeling well today.*

Rule 4b. A **weak clause** begins with words such as *although, since, if, when,* and *because.* Weak clauses cannot stand on their own.

Examples: *Although* <u>she</u> <u>is</u> *hungry...*
If <u>she</u> <u>is</u> *hungry...*
Since <u>I</u> <u>am feeling</u> *well...*

Rule 4c. If a sentence contains more than one clause, isolate the clauses so that you can decide which pronoun is correct.

Examples:	Weak	Strong
	[Although <u>she</u> <u>is</u> hungry,]	[<u>she</u> <u>will give</u> him some of her food.]
	[Although this <u>gift</u> <u>is</u> for him,]	[<u>I</u> <u>would like</u> you to have it too.]

Rule 5. To decide whether to use the Subject or Object pronoun after the words *than* or *as*, mentally complete the sentence.

Examples: *Tranh is as smart as she/her.*
If we mentally complete the sentence, we would say, "Tranh is as smart as she is." Therefore, *she* is the correct answer.
Zoe is taller than I/me.
Mentally completing the sentence, we have, "Zoe is taller than I am."
Daniel would rather talk to her than I/me.
We can mentally complete this sentence in two ways: "Daniel would rather talk to her than to me." **OR** "Daniel would rather talk to her than I would." As you can see, the meaning will change depending on the pronoun you choose.

Rule 6. Possessive pronouns show ownership and never need apostrophes. Possessive pronouns: *mine, yours, his, hers, its, ours,* and *theirs*

Note

The only time *it's* has an apostrophe is when it is a contraction for *it is* or *it has*.

Examples: *It's a cold morning.*
The thermometer reached its highest reading.

Rule 7. Reflexive pronouns—*myself, himself, herself, itself, themselves, ourselves, yourself, yourselves*—should be used only when they refer back to another word in the sentence.

Correct: *I did it myself.*
Incorrect: *My brother and myself did it.*

The word *myself* does not refer back to another word.

Correct: *My brother and I did it.*

Incorrect: *Please give it to John or myself.*

Correct: *Please give it to John or me.*

Who vs. Whom

<u>Rule.</u> Use the *he/him* method to decide which word is correct.

he = who

him = whom

Examples: **Who**/*Whom wrote the letter?*

He wrote the letter. Therefore, *who* is correct.

*For who/**whom** should I vote?*

Should I vote for him? Therefore, *whom* is correct.

*We all know **who**/whom pulled that prank.*

This sentence contains two clauses: *We all know* and *who/whom pulled that prank.* We are interested in the second clause because it contains the *who/whom. He pulled that prank.* Therefore, *who* is correct. (Are you starting to sound like a hooting owl yet?)

*We want to know on who/**whom** the prank was pulled.*

This sentence contains two clauses: *We want to know* and *the prank was pulled on who/whom.* Again, we are interested in the second clause because it contains the *who/whom.* The prank was pulled on him. Therefore, *whom* is correct.

Whoever vs. Whomever

<u>Rule 1.</u> To determine whether to use *whoever* or *whomever*, here is the rule:

him + he = whoever

him + him = whomever

*Example: Give it to whoever/**whomever** asks for it first.*

Give it to *him. He* asks for it first.

Therefore, *Give it to **whoever** asks for it first.*

*Example: We will hire whoever/**whomever** you recommend.*

We will hire *him.* You recommend *him.*

him + him = whomever

*Example: We will hire **whoever**/whomever is most qualified.*
  We will hire him. He is most qualified.
  him + he = whoever

<u>Rule 2.</u> When the entire *whoever/whomever* clause is the subject of the verb that follows the clause, look inside the clause to determine whether to use *whoever* or *whomever*.

Example: Whoever is elected will serve a four-year term.
  Whoever is elected is the subject of will serve.
Example: Whomever you elect will serve a four-year term.
  Whomever you elect is the subject of will serve.
  Whomever is the object of you elect.

That vs. Which

<u>Rule 1.</u> *Who* refers to people. *That* and *which* refer to groups or things.

*Examples: Anya is the one **who** rescued the bird.*
  *Lokua is on the team **that** won first place.*
  *She belongs to an organization **that** specializes in saving endangered species.*

<u>Rule 2.</u> *That* introduces essential clauses while *which* introduces nonessential clauses.

*Examples: I do not trust editorials **that** claim racial differences in intelligence.*
  We would not know which editorials were being discussed without the *that* clause.
  *The editorial claiming racial differences in intelligence, **which** appeared in the Sunday newspaper, upset me.*
  The editorial is already identified. Therefore, *which* begins a nonessential clause.

Note

Essential clauses do not have commas surrounding them while nonessential clauses are surrounded by commas.

<u>Rule 3.</u> If *this, that, these,* and *those* have already introduced an essential clause, you may use *which* to introduce the next clause, whether it is essential or nonessential.

Examples: **That** *is a decision* **which** *you must live with for the rest of your life.*

Those ideas, **which** *we've discussed thoroughly enough, do not need to be addressed again.*

Note

Often, you can streamline your sentence by leaving out *which*.

Example: **Those** *ideas,* **which** *we have discussed thoroughly, do not need to be addressed again.*

Better: *The ideas we have discussed thoroughly do not need to be addressed again.*

Example: **That** *is a decision* **which** *you must live with for the rest of your life.*

Better: **That** *is a decision you must live with for the rest of your life.*

OR

You must live with **that** *decision for the rest of your life.*

Adjectives and Adverbs

Definitions: Adjectives are words that describe nouns or pronouns. They may come before the word they describe (That is a *cute* puppy.) or they may follow the word they describe (That puppy is *cute*.).

<u>Rule 1.</u> Adverbs are words that modify everything but nouns and pronouns. They modify adjectives, verbs, and other adverbs. A word is an adverb if it answers *how, when,* or *where.* The only adverbs that cause grammatical problems are those that answer the question *how,* so focus on these.

Example: He speaks **slowly***.*

Answers the question *how.*

Example: He speaks **very** *slowly.*

Answers the question *how slowly.*

<u>Rule 2.</u> Generally, if a word answers the question *how,* it is an adverb. If it can have an *-ly* added to it, place it there.

*Examples: She thinks slow/***slowly***.*

She thinks *how?* slowly.

She is a **slow***/slowly thinker.*

Slow does not answer *how,* so no *-ly* is attached. *Slow* is an adjective here.

She thinks **fast***/fastly.*

Fast answers the question *how,* so it is an adverb. But *fast* never has an *-ly* attached to it.

*We performed bad/**badly**.*

Badly describes *how* we performed.

Rule 3. A special *-ly* rule applies when four of the senses—*taste, smell, look, feel*—are the verbs. Do not ask if these senses answer the question *how* to determine if *-ly* should be attached. Instead, ask if the sense verb is being used actively. If so, use the *-ly*.

Examples: *Roses smell **sweet**/sweetly.*

Do the roses actively smell with noses? No, so no *-ly*.

*The woman looked **angry**/angrily.*

Did the woman actively look with eyes or are we describing her appearance? We are only describing appearance, so no *-ly*.

*The woman looked angry/**angrily** at the paint splotches.*

Here the woman did actively look with eyes, so the *-ly* is added.

*She feels **bad**/badly about the news.*

She is not feeling with fingers, so no *-ly*.

Good vs. Well

Rule 4. The word *good* is an adjective, while *well* is an adverb.

Examples: *You did a good job.*

Good describes the job.

You did the job well.

Well answers how.

You smell good today.

Describes your odor, not how you smell with your nose, so follow with the adjective.

You smell well for someone with a cold.

You are actively smelling with a nose here, so follow with the adverb.

Rule 5. When referring to health, use *well* rather than *good*.

Examples: *I do not feel well.*

You do not look well today.

Note

You may use *good* with *feel* when you are not referring to health.

Example: *I feel good about my decision to learn Spanish.*

<u>**Rule 6.**</u> A common error in using adjectives and adverbs arises from using the wrong form for comparison. For instance, to describe one thing we would say *poor*, as in, "She is *poor*." To compare two things, we should say *poorer*, as in, "She is the *poorer* of the two women." To compare more than two things, we should say *poorest*, as in, "She is the *poorest* of them all."

Examples:	**One**	**Two**	**Three or More**
	sweet	*sweeter*	*sweetest*
	bad	*worse*	*worst*
	*efficient**	*more efficient**	*most efficient**

Note

Usually with words of three or more syllables, don't add –*er* or –*est*.
Use *more* or *most* in front of the words.

<u>**Rule 7.**</u> Never drop the -*ly* from an adverb when using the comparison form.

Correct: *She spoke quickly.*
        She spoke more quickly than he did.
Incorrect: *She spoke quicker than he did.*
Correct: *Talk quietly.*
        Talk more quietly.
Incorrect: *Talk quieter.*

<u>**Rule 8.**</u> When *this, that, these,* and *those* are followed by nouns, they are adjectives. When they appear without a noun following them, they are pronouns.

Examples: *This house is for sale.*
        This is an adjective here.
        This is for sale.
        This is a pronoun here.

<u>**Rule 9.**</u> *This* and *that* are singular, whether they are being used as adjectives or as pronouns. *This* points to something nearby, while *that* points to something "over there."

Examples: *This dog is mine.*
        That dog is hers.
        This is mine.
        That is hers.

Rule 10. *These* and *those* are plural, whether they are being used as adjectives or as pronouns. *These* points to something nearby while *those* points to something "over there."

> *Examples: These babies have been smiling for a long time.*
> *These are mine.*
> *Those babies have been crying for hours.*
> *Those are yours.*

Rule 11. Use *than* to show comparison. Use *then* to answer the question *when*.

> *Examples: I would rather go skiing than rock climbing.*
> *First we went skiing; then we went rock climbing.*

Problems with Prepositions

Rule 1. You may end a sentence with a preposition. Just do not use extra prepositions when the meaning is clear without them.

> *Examples:*
> *Correct:*   *That is something I cannot agree with.*
>   *That is something with which I cannot agree.*
> *Correct:*   *How many of you can I count on?*
> *Correct:*   *Where did he go?*
> *Incorrect: Where did he go to?*
> *Correct:*   *Where did you get this?*
> *Incorrect: Where did you get this at?*
> *Correct:*   *I will go later.*
> *Incorrect: I will go later on.*
> *Correct:*   *Take your shoes off the bed.*
> *Incorrect: Take your shoes off of the bed.*
> *Correct:*   *You may look out the window.*
> *Incorrect: You may look out of the window.*
> *Correct:*   *Cut it into small pieces.*
> *Incorrect: Cut it up into small pieces.*

Rule 2. Use *on* with expressions that indicate the time of an occurrence.

> *Examples: He was born on December 23.*
> *We will arrive on the fourth.*

Rule 3. *Of* should never be used in place of *have*.

> *Correct:*   *I should have done it.*
> *Incorrect: I should of done it.*

<u>**Rule 4.**</u> *Between* refers to two. *Among* is used for three or more.

> *Examples: Divide the candy between the two of you.*
> *Divide the candy among the three of you.*

<u>**Rule 5.**</u> *Into* implies entrance; *in* does not.

> *Examples: Sofia walked into the house.*
> *Sofia was waiting in the house.*
> *Miriam came in to see me today.*
> *In* is part of the verb phrase *came in*, while *to* is part of *to see.*

<u>**Rule 6.**</u> The word *like*, when used to show comparison, is a preposition, meaning that it should be followed by an object of the preposition but not by a subject and verb. Use the connectors (also called conjunctions) *as* or *as if* when following a comparison with a subject and verb.

> *Examples: You look so much like your mother.*
> *Mother* is the object of the preposition *like.*
> *You look as if you are angry.*
> *As if* is connecting two pairs of subjects and verbs.

Effective Writing

<u>**Rule 1.**</u> Use concrete rather than vague language.

> *Examples:*
> **Vague:**   *The weather was of an extreme nature on the west coast.*
> **Concrete:** *California had very cold weather last week.*

<u>**Rule 2.**</u> Use active voice whenever possible. Active voice means the subject is performing the verb.

> *Examples:*
> **Active:** *Barry hit the ball.*
> **Passive:** *The ball was hit.*

Notice that the responsible party may not even appear when using passive voice.

<u>**Rule 3.**</u> Avoid overusing *there is, there are, it is, it was*, and so on.

> **Example:**   *There is a case of meningitis that was reported in the newspaper.*
> **Correction:** *A case of meningitis was reported in the newspaper.*
> **Even Better:** *The newspaper reported a case of meningitis.* (Active voice)

Example: *It is important to signal before making a left turn.*
Correction: *Signaling before making a left turn is important.*
      OR
      Signaling before a left turn is important.
      OR
      You should signal before making a left turn. (Active voice)
Example: *There are some revisions which must be made.*
Correction: *Some revisions must be made.*
Even Better: *Please make some revisions.* (Active voice)

<u>**Rule 4.**</u> To avoid confusion, don't use two negatives to make a positive.

> *Incorrect: He is not unwilling to help.*
>
> *Correct: He is willing to help.*

<u>**Rule 5.**</u> Use similar grammatical form when offering several ideas. This is called parallel construction.

> *Correct: You should check your spelling, grammar, and punctuation.*
>
> *Incorrect: You should check your spelling, grammar, and punctuating.*

<u>**Rule 6.**</u> If you start a sentence with an action, place the actor immediately after or you will have created the infamous dangling modifier.

> *Incorrect: While walking across the street, the bus hit her.*
>
> *Correct: While walking across the street, she was hit by a bus.*
>
>   **OR**
>
> *She was hit by a bus while walking across the street.*

<u>**Rule 7.**</u> Place modifiers near the words they modify.

> *Incorrect: I have some pound cake Mollie baked in my lunch bag.*
>
> *Correct: In my lunch bag, I have some pound cake that Mollie baked.*

<u>**Rule 8.**</u> A sentence fragment occurs when you have only a phrase or weak clause but are missing a strong clause.

> *Example of Sentence Fragment: After the show ended.*
>
> *Example of Sentence:*   *After the show ended, we had*
>   *coffee.*

Chapter 2

Confusing Words and Homonyms

Because many words in English sound or look alike, frequently causing confusion, this list will be very helpful.

a vs. an

<u>Rule</u>. Use *a* when the first letter of the word following has the sound of a consonant. Keep in mind that some vowels sound like consonants when they're sounded out as individual letters.

Examples:

- *a finger*
- *a hotel*
- *a U-turn* (pronounced Yoo-turn)
- *a HUD program*
- *a NASA study*

<u>Rule</u>. Use *an* when the first letter of the word following has the sound of a vowel. Remember that some consonants sound like vowels when they're spoken as individual letters.

Examples:

- *an FBI case* (*F* is pronounced *ef* here)
- *an honor* (*H* is silent here)
- *an unusual idea*
- *an HMO plan* (*H* is pronounced *aych* here)
- *an NAACP convention* (*N* is pronounced *en* here)

Deciding whether to use *a* or *an* before abbreviations can be tricky. The abbreviation for Frequently Asked Questions (FAQ) causes confusion because it can be pronounced as a word (fak), or one letter at a time (F-A-Q). Using the guidelines above, one would say *a FAQ* when it is pronounced as one word, and *an FAQ* when it is pronounced one letter at a time.

accept	to agree
except	but, with the exception that

ad	advertisement
add	to perform addition

ades	fruit drinks
aides	people who help; assistants
AIDS	acronym for Acquired Immune Deficiency Syndrome
aids	helps, assists

adverse   unfortunate; strongly opposed (refers to things, not people)

> ***Examples:*** *an adverse reaction to the medication*
> *adverse weather conditions*

averse   having repugnance (refers to people)

> ***Example:*** *He is averse to a military draft.*

advice vs. advise

advice (noun)	recommendation
advise (verb)	the act of giving a recommendation

affect vs. effect

Rule 1. Use *effect* when you mean *bring about* or *brought about, cause* or *caused.*

> ***Example:*** *He effected a commotion in the crowd.*
> ***Meaning:*** *He caused a commotion in the crowd.*

Rule 2. Use *effect* when you mean *result.*

> ***Example:*** *What effect did that speech have?*

Rule 3. Also use *effect* whenever any of these words precede it: *a, an, the, any, take, into, no.* These words may be separated from *effect* by an adjective.

> ***Examples:*** *That book had a long-lasting effect on my thinking.*
> *Has the medicine produced any noticeable effects?*

Rule 4. Use the verb *affect* when you mean *to influence* rather than *to cause.*

> ***Example:*** *How do the budget cuts affect your staffing?*

Rule 5. *Affect* is used as a noun to mean *emotional expression*.

> *Example: She showed little affect when told she had won the lottery.*

ail	to be ill; to cause pain or distress
ale	malt beverage more bitter than beer
air	what we breathe
err	make a mistake
heir	one who inherits something
aisle	passageway
I'll	contraction for *I will*
isle	a small island
all	entire, everything
awl	a tool
allot	to parcel out
a lot	always two words meaning *many*
allowed	gave permission to
aloud	said out loud; spoken
all ready	means *all are ready*

> *Example: We are all ready to go.*

already	refers to time

> *Example: Is it summer already?*

all together	refers to a group; all of us or all of them together

> *Example: It is wonderful to be all together to celebrate your birthday.*

altogether	entirely

> *Example: It is not altogether his fault.*

altar	pedestal, usually religious

> *Example: They exchanged wedding vows at the altar of the church.*

alter	to modify

> *Example: Please don't alter your plans until we have the final schedule approved.*

allude   to refer indirectly

Example: *He alluded to his past as a spy.*

elude   avoid capture

Example: *The fugitive eluded the police for a month.*

illude   mislead

Example: *He illuded her about his age.*

---

allusion   an indirect mention of something
illusion   false perception

---

ambiguous   to have more than one meaning

Example: *The law was ambiguous.*

ambivalent   to have mixed feelings

Example: *She is ambivalent about her wedding dress.*

---

amicable   friendly (refers to things, not people)
amiable   friendly (refers to people)

Example: *The amiable couple had an amicable divorce.*

---

among   involves three or more

Example: *Who among us has not lied?*

between   involves just two

Example: *She couldn't decide between Chinese and Thai food.*

---

amount   used for things not countable

Example: *We couldn't handle that amount of ill will.*

number   used for things that can be counted

Example: *The number of accidents increased by ten percent.*

---

ant   a bug
aunt   the sister of a parent

---

ante   a bet placed before playing
auntie   affectionate term for a parent's sister

anxious   to have anxiety or worry

   Example: She is anxious about taking the test.

eager   excited

   Example: She is eager to get a puppy.

---

any more   something additional or further

   Example: It didn't rain any more this year than last year.

anymore   any longer, nowadays

   Example: Harry doesn't travel anymore.

---

appraise	to put a value on something
apprise	to notify

---

arc	arch, crescent, half moon
ark	a vessel or a refuge

---

ascent (noun)	movement upward
assent (noun or verb)	enthusiastic agreement; to agree
consent	agreement

---

assistance (noun)	help
assistants (noun)	people who help

---

assumption	an idea not based on evidence
presumption	an idea based on evidence

---

assure	to promise or say with confidence
ensure	to make sure something will/won't happen
insure	to issue an insurance policy

---

ate	past tense of *eat*
eight	the number after *seven*

---

aural	having to do with hearing
oral	having to do with the mouth

---

averse	(see *adverse*)

awed	in a state of amazement
odd	unusual; opposite of *even* when referring to numbers
aye	yes
eye	organ one sees with
I	pronoun
bald	having no hair
bawled	cried
ball	a sphere
bawl	to cry or wail loudly
band	a group, sometimes a group of musicians
banned	forbidden
bare	naked, unconcealed, plain
bear	the animal
base	the bottom; vulgar; headquarters (singular)
bass	low vocal or instrumental range (pronounced like *lace*); a type of fish (pronounced like *lass*)
based	be dependent or supported
baste	to moisten; to criticize or lash out at
bases (noun, verb)	headquarters (plural of *base*); builds on
basis (noun)	foundation; belief
be	to exist or live
bee	insect
beach	sandy area with water
beech	type of tree with smooth, gray bark
beat	to strike violently; to flutter or flap; to pound as with a drum; to defeat; to stir vigorously
beet	a plant with a fleshy red or white root
beau	boyfriend (pronounced like *owe*)
bough	branch of a tree (pronounced like *cow*)
bow (noun)	part of a set with arrows (pronounced like *owe*)
bow (noun, verb)	boat front; a male's form of curtsy, bending at the waist; comply (pronounced like *cow*)

because vs. since

<u>Rule</u>. *Because* and *since* can be used almost interchangeably although *because* always indicates cause and effect and *since* is used for a relationship or time.

> *Example: Since I have some extra money, I will buy shoes.* (not cause and effect)
> *Example: I will go to the game because my daughter is on the team.* (cause and effect)
> *Example: I have wanted to talk to you since yesterday.* (time)

been	form of *be* used with *has* or *have*
bin	container
bell	chime or alarm; a signal
belle	beautiful or charming woman
berth	a boat dock; bedroom or bed
birth	being born; beginning
better	of higher quality
bettor	someone who places bets
between	(see *among*)
biannual	twice a year
biennial	every two years
semiannual	twice a year (same as *biannual*)
bite	to use one's teeth to tear food
byte	computer term for eight bits of information
billed	charged a fee
build	construct
blew	past tense of *blow*
blue	the color
bloc	a group united for a particular purpose
block	city street; a cube-shaped object
boar	male pig
bore	someone or something not interesting
board	piece of wood; a group of people
bored	uninterested

boarder	someone who pays for room and food
border	perimeter; boundary
bode	predict
bowed	bent (pronounced like *owed)*
bold	daring
bowled	to have gone bowling; knocked over
bolder	more daring
boulder	a large rock
boos	sounds made by disapproving audience
booze	alcohol
bough	(see *beau)*
bow	(see *beau)*
boy	male child
buoy	a naval beacon or marker
brake	stop
break	separate into pieces
bread	a food; slang for *money*
bred	past tense of *breed*; raised
brewed	fermented
brood (verb, noun)	mull over; a cluster or family
brews	ferments
bruise	a black-and-blue mark, contusion
bridal	relating to brides
bridle	a harness, usually for a horse
bring	you bring something towards
take	you take something away
broach	to raise a topic
brooch	a bauble; a piece of jewelry
brows	the hairs in the arch above the eyes
browse	search for, peruse
but	except
butt (noun/verb)	bottom; joke object; to ram

buy	purchase, acquire
by	near, next to
bye	short for *goodbye*
cache	hidden stash
cash	money
calendar	chart of days and months
colander	sieve to drain off liquids
can	able to
may	permission to
cannon	large, mounted gun
canon	rule, commandment
canvas	awning cloth, tarp
canvass	to poll; a poll
capital	assets; essential; main city
capitol	statehouse
carat	unit of weight in gemstones
caret	a proofreading mark to show insertion (∧)
carrot	edible root
karat	a unit for measuring the fineness of gold
cast (noun, verb)	group of actors; to throw
caste	a social class, a rigid system of social distinctions
cay	a small, low island (also spelled *key*)
key	a small, low island; instrument for opening locks
quay	(pronounced *key)* wharf, dock, pier
cede	to surrender
seed	reproductive germ
cell	prison room; basic structural unit of an organism
sell	to exchange for money

censor (verb, noun)	disallow; person who disallows

Example: The soldier's letters were censored before mailing.

censure	to disapprove of; criticize strongly

Example: The children were censured by the principal.

sensor	a device that measures heat, light, etc. and transmits a signal to a control or measuring instrument

cent	a penny
scent	a smell, aroma
sent	transmitted

cereal	breakfast food
serial	a series or array

chance	accident(al)
chants	chorus, melody

chased	went after
chaste	pure, virginal

chews	how one eats food with teeth
choose	to pick

childish	immature
childlike	innocent

Chile	a country in South America
chili	a type of pepper; a dish with peppers in it
chilly	cold, brisk

choral	a cappella, singing without instruments
coral	material that makes up reefs; orange color
chorale	a hymn, a choir
corral	horse pen

chord	three or more musical tones sounded simultaneously; line segment joining two points on a curve
cord	a rope or strand of flexible material
cored	removed the center of something

chute	an inclined shaft
shoot (verb, noun)	to discharge from a weapon; a stem
cite	to assert; to quote from; to subpoena
sight	vision, the power to see
site	a location or position
classic	important; fundamental
classical	having to do with Greek or Roman antiquity; pertaining to eighteenth- to nineteenth-century music
clause	in grammar, a group of words containing a subject and verb; part of a contract
claws	an animal's nails
click	a sound
clique	a group
climactic	having to do with the climax
climatic	having to do with the climate
close (verb, adjective)	to shut (pronounced like *rose*); nearby (pronounced like *dose)*
clothes	apparel
coarse	rough, lacking in fineness of texture; crude
course	a class; a path
colander	(see *calendar)*
colonel	an officer in the military
kernel	a seed
complement	completing part of an order
compliment	praise
confidant	someone confided in
confident	certain, sure
connote	to suggest, infer

Example: A roaring fire in the fireplace connotes a cozy winter night.

denote	to be a sign of

Example: Certain clouds denote rain on the way.

consent	(see *assent*)
continual	repeated but with breaks in between; chronic

Example: The continual problem of our car not starting forced us to sell it.

continuous	without interruption in an unbroken stream of time or space

Example: The continuous dripping of the faucet drove me crazy.

core	center or crucial part
corps	trained group
corpse	dead body
cosign	to sign along with
cosine	a trigonometry term
council	a group of people meeting for a purpose
counsel (verb, noun)	advise; advice, an attorney
creak	a sound
creek	a stream
crews	many groups
cruise	a trip or vacation by sea
criteria	plural of *criterion*
criterion	a standard for evaluating or testing something
cue	a hint; a stimulus
queue	a line of people waiting
currant	type of small berry
current	up to date
curser	someone who swears or wishes misfortune on another
cursor	a blinking symbol indicating position on a computer screen
dam	a barrier obstructing the flow of liquid
damn	a swear word or curse
dammed	blocked from flowing
damned	doomed

days	twenty-four-hour periods of time
daze	to stun or overwhelm
dear	affectionate term
deer	the animal
denote	(see *connote)*
desert (noun, verb)	a desolate area; to abandon
dessert	extra *s* for sugary treat
desperate	lost all hope, in despair
disparate	entirely dissimilar
device (noun)	an invention
devise (verb)	to invent
dew	condensation in the morning
do	to take action
due	owed by a certain date
die	to cease to live; the singular of *dice*
dye	to stain or color using an agent

different from vs. differently than

Rule. Use *different from,* not *different than.*

Example: The weather was different from what we expected.

You may use *differently than* when a clause precedes and follows the expression.

Example: He works differently than she does.

discreet	careful, confidential
discrete	individual, distinct
discussed	talked over
disgust	repulsion
does	female deer (plural) (pronounced like *hose)*
does	a form of *to do* (pronounced like *fuzz)*
doughs	unbaked loaves of bread
doze	to sleep

dual	two-fold
duel	fight

eager	(see *anxious*)

effect	(see *affect*)

e.g.	for example

Example: My living expenses have increased, e.g., rent, food, and utilities.

i.e.	that is, in other words

Example: My living expenses have drained my finances; i.e., I have less money in the bank at the end of every month.

eight	(see *ate*)

elicit	evoke, extract, draw out
illicit	illegal

elude	(see *allude*)

elusive	difficult to describe, evasive

Example: The point of the novel is elusive to me.

illusive	plausible or possible; deceptive

Example: She had the illusive dream of finding happiness by traveling. (plausible, possible)

Example: She had an illusive idea that she was qualified for the job. (deceptive, delusional)

emigrate	to exit one country in order to live in another country
immigrate	to enter a new country to live

empathy	to understand another's feelings
sympathy	to feel compassion or sadness for another

ensure	(see *assure*)

epic	saga
epoch	a period of time, an age

err	(see *air*)

every day   each day

    Example: I learn something new every day.

everyday   ordinary

    Example: These are my everyday clothes.

except	(see *accept*)
eye	(see *aye*)
facts	objective data
fax	short for *facsimile*; technology that sends images by phone
faint	to go unconscious
feint	pretense
fair (adjective, noun)	impartial; an exhibition
fare	payment or expense for travel
fairy	imaginary being possessing magical powers
ferry	type of boat

farther   refers to physical distance

    Example: We had to walk farther than the map indicated.

further   refers to nonphysical distance

    Examples: We need to discuss this further.
               Nothing could be further from the truth.

faux	fake, imitation
foe	enemy, opponent
faze	to perturb or fluster
phase	a period or situation
feat	an extraordinary act or accomplishment
feet	twelve-inch increments; appendages at end of legs
feted	celebrated, honored
fetid	noxious, gross

fewer   refers to a number that can be counted

    Example: Fewer days off.

less   refers to an uncountable amount

    Examples: Less rain, less fear, less than $100.

under   used for direction

    Examples: Under the mattress, not under $100.

find	discover
fined	penalized
fir	type of tree
fur	hairy coat of an animal
flair	style
flare	erupt
flea	insect
flee	to run away
flew	past tense of *fly*, to have moved through the air with wings
flu	a virus
flue	part of a chimney
floe	sheet of floating ice
flow	pour, proceed, spew
flour	grain
flower	the bloom of a plant
for	preposition
fore	ahead
four	the number after *three*
forego	to go in front of, precede
forgo	to do without
foreword	introduction to a book written by someone other than the author
forward	opposite of *backward*
fort	a military fortification
forte	someone's strong point, talent
forth	forward
fourth	number after *third*

foul	offensive, disgusting
fowl	certain birds
frees	releases
freeze	to make cold
frieze	a decorative band on a wall
further	(see *farther*)
gait	a manner of walking or stepping, stride

Examples: trotting, galloping, limping

gate	barrier
gilt	gold-covered
guilt	blame
gone	used with *has* or *have*

Examples: *Ella has gone to the store.*
              Barry and Ella have gone to the beach.

went	past tense of go

Examples: *Ella went to the store.*
           Barry and Ella went to the beach.

gored	stabbed with a horn or tusk
gourd	hard-shelled fruit
gorilla	largest of the apes
guerrilla	soldier using surprise raids; irregular tactics
graft	attach; acquisition of money dishonestly
graphed	diagrammed
grate	a cover or partition of parallel or crossed bars
great	excellent
grill	method of cooking; barbecuing
grille	an openwork barrier for a gate
groan	a low, mournful sound of pain or grief
grown	to have increased in size
guessed	conjectured, offered an opinion
guest	company, honoree
guise	appearance or assumed appearance
guys	men

hair	what grows on one's head and body
hare	rabbit
hall	passageway or large room
haul	to pull, drag, or lower
halve	divide into two
have	to possess
hangar	shed or shelter for housing airplanes
hanger	something to hang a garment on in the closet
haut/haute	high-class, fancy as in haute couture (pronounced *oh* or *oht*)
hoe	flat-bladed gardening tool
have vs. of	*should've, could've,* and *would've* are contractions for *should have, could have,* and *would have.* No such wording as *should of, could of, would of*
hay	dried grass
hey	interjection used to call attention
heal	to alleviate or cure
heel	the back part of the foot; scoundrel
healthful	something that promotes health

Example: *Organic food is thought to be healthful.*

healthy	to have good health
hear	to listen; to give an official hearing
here	in this spot
heard	listened
herd	a flock of animals
heir	(see *air*)
heroin	a narcotic derived from morphine
heroine	female admired for courage or ability
hi	a greeting; informal for *hello*
high	elevated
higher	more elevated
hire	to pay for services

him	pronoun referring to male person or animal
hymn	song in praise of religious deity
hoard	stockpile, amass
horde	a large group, crowd
hoarse	cracked voice
horse	animal
hoes	flat-bladed gardening tools
hose	a flexible tube for conveying liquid
hole	an opening
whole	entire, complete
holy	religious
wholly	entirely, completely
hostel	boarding house or inexpensive lodging
hostile	antagonistic
hour	sixty minutes
our	possessive pronoun
I	(see *aye*)
idle	not active; unemployed
idol	someone admired
idyll	interlude, breathing space; romance, fairy tale
i.e.	(see *e.g.*)
I'll	(see *aisle*)
illicit	(see *elicit*)
illude	(see *allude*)
illusion	(see *allusion*)
illusive	(see *elusive*)
immigrate	(see *emigrate*)
imply	to indicate without being explicit
infer	to conclude from evidence
in	preposition; inside
inn	small hotel

Inc.	abbreviation for *incorporated*
ink	fluid in pens

incite	to prompt to action
insight	understanding, comprehension

incredible	astonishing

Example: Her gymnastic moves were incredible.

incredulous	skeptical

Example: Citizens are incredulous about the reason for the increase in the price of gas.

ingenious	clever
ingenuous	naïve or simple

innocence	to be without guilt
innocents	people who are without guilt

insure	(see *assure*)

irregardless	no such word exists
regardless	in spite of, without regard

isle	(see *aisle*)

it's	contraction for *it is* or *it has*

Example: It's for a good cause.

its	possessive pronoun

Example: The cat hurt its paw.

jewel	gem
joule	in physics, a unit of work or energy

karat	(see *carat*)

kernel	(see *colonel*)

key	(see *cay*)

knead	work with bread dough
kneed	hit with one's knee
need	to require

knight	a soldier in the Middle Ages
night	period between sunset and sunrise

knot	interlacing of cord or rope
not	used to express negation
knew	past tense of *know*, to have understood
new	opposite of *old*
know	understand, comprehend
no	a negative to express dissent
knows	understands
nose	part of the body one smells with
lacks	is deficient in
lax	slack, easy-going
ladder	the thing with rungs that you climb
latter	the second of two

Example: If given a choice between vanilla and chocolate ice cream, I'll take the latter.

lain	past participle of *lie* as in *lie down*
lane	narrow road or passage

lay vs. lie chart

	Present	Past	Participle (A Form of Have)
To recline	lie, lying	lay	has/have/had lain
To put or place (verb followed by an object)	lay, laying	laid	has/have/had laid
To tell a falsehood	lie, lying	lied	has/have/had lied

Examples in the Present Tense:
I like to lie down for a nap at 2:00 P.M.
I am lying down for a nap today.
The hens lay eggs.
The hen is laying eggs.
I am tempted to lie about my age.
I am not lying about my age.

Examples in the Past Tense:
I lay down for a nap yesterday at 2:00 P.M.
The hen laid two eggs yesterday.
He lied on the witness stand.

Examples with a Participle (has, have):
I have lain down for a nap every day this week.
The hen has laid two eggs every day this week.
He has lied each day on the witness stand.

lead	a metal element (pronounced like *red*); present tense of *led* (pronounced like *seed*)
led	guided, past tense of *to lead*
leak	unintended discharge of liquid or gas
leek	type of onion
lean (adjective, verb)	not fatty; to incline
lien	a claim on property to secure debt payment
leased	rented
least	smallest in size or amount
less	(see *fewer*)
lessen	to make less
lesson	a unit to be learned or studied
lie	a falsehood; present tense of *lie down* (see *lay vs. lie* chart above)
lye	a caustic substance
lightening	to make lighter
lightning	a brilliant electric spark in the sky
loan	something lent for temporary use
lone	only, solitary
loose	opposite of *tight*
lose	opposite of *win*; misplace
Mach	ratio with the speed of sound: Mach 1 = the speed of sound Mach 2 = twice the speed of sound
mock (adjective, verb)	artificial; ridicule
made	created
maid	cleaning lady
mail	correspondence
male	masculine; opposite of *female*

main	primary, chief, leading
mane	long hair on the back of a horse or lion
maize	corn
maze	labyrinth
mall	plaza, focal point
maul	abuse, claw
manner	behavior
manor	palatial residence
marquee	canopy, shelter; projection over a theater entrance
marquis	aristocrat, nobleman
marry	to wed
merry	cheerful
marshal (verb, noun)	assemble; a judge
martial	militant, aggressive
may	(see *can*)
meat	animal flesh used for food
meet (verb, noun)	to connect, touch; an event
mete	administer, allot
medal	decoration, badge
meddle	to interfere unwantedly
metal	earth element
mettle	boldness
mind (noun, verb)	intelligence; obey
mined	excavated to extract ores
miner	one who excavates to extract ores
minor (noun, adjective)	someone under legal age; small
missed	failed to hit
mist	fog, fine spray
moan	lament; sound of suffering
mown	cut grass
mode	method, manner
mowed	to have cut grass

mood	an emotional state
mooed	the sound a cow made
moose	an animal
mousse	type of dessert
morning	start of the day, between night and afternoon
mourning	sorrow over someone's death
muscle	fibrous tissue
mussel	edible marine bivalve
mustard	yellow condiment
mustered	assembled, gathered
naval	pertaining to ships
navel	belly button, umbilicus
need	(see *knead*)
new	(see *knew*)
night	(see *knight*)
no	(see *know*)
none	not one, not any
nun	female member of a religious order
nose	(see *knows*)
not	(see *knot*)
number	(see *amount*)
oar	a blade for rowing
or	conjunction
ore	metal-bearing mineral or rock
odd	(see *awed*)
of	(see *have*)
on to vs. onto	Use *onto* if you can add *up* before *on*.

Examples: He climbed (up) onto the roof.
         She held on to her child in the crowd.

one	single unit
won	past tense of *win*
oral	(see *aural*)
ordinance	a law
ordnance	military weapons and ammunition
our	(see *hour*)
overdo	to do to excess
overdue	past due
packed	past tense of *pack*
pact	an agreement or treaty
pail	bucket
pale	lacking color
pain	physical or emotional suffering
pane	a plate of glass or panel
pair	two of something
pare	to remove or peel
pear	type of fruit
palate	roof of the mouth; taste
pallet	a low, portable platform
palette	a range of colors; a board to hold and mix colors
passed	past tense of *pass*
past	the time before the present
patience	willingness to wait
patients	people under medical care
pause	a temporary stop
paws	animal feet
peace	calm
piece	a portion of something
peak	top of a mountain
peek	glance furtively
pique	to wound someone's pride or to excite interest

pealed	rang bells
peeled	removed a layer
pedal	foot-operated lever
peddle	to sell, hawk, or dispense
peer	person who is an equal
pier	a structure extending out over water
perpetrate	to commit, as in a crime
perpetuate	to prolong or sustain

Example: The myth that the sun revolved around the earth was perpetuated for centuries.

phase	(see *faze*)
pi	3.1416, the ratio of the circumference of a circle to its diameter
pie	baked food filled with fruit or meat
pistil	female organ of a flower
pistol	type of gun
plain (adjective, noun)	not fancy; evident; simple; treeless area of land
plane	a flat or level surface; short for *airplane*
pleas	cries for help; appeals
please	a polite word; to satisfy
plum	a type of fruit
plumb	perpendicular
pole	a long, cylindrical piece of wood or metal
poll	a collection of opinions; survey
pore	small hole
pour	to send liquid flowing
praise	express approval
prays	makes requests to God
preys	hunts for food; victimizes
precedence	priority
precedents	examples, criteria
presidents	chief executives

presence	appearance, being present
presents (noun, verb)	gifts; offers
presumption	(see *assumption*)
pries	looks closely; wedges open
prize	award or reward
principal (noun, adjective)	head of school; chief; of first importance
principle	fundamental belief
profit	gain
prophet	predictor, seer
pros	professionals, experts
prose	literature
quarts	units of liquid measure (four quarts to a gallon)
quartz	a mineral
quay	(see *cay*)
queue	(see *cue*)
rain	water that falls in drops from the sky
reign	rule, administration
rein	bit, harness
raise	lift up
raze	flatten, tear down completely
rap (noun, verb)	a type of music; to strike sharply
wrap	to enclose in a covering
rapped	struck sharply
rapt	fascinated
wrapped	enclosed in a covering
read	present and past tenses of *to comprehend writing*
red	a color
real	actual, authentic
reel	stumble, falter

recede	to move back, withdraw
reseed	to seed again
reek	to smell bad
wreak	to cause trouble as in *wreak havoc*
regardless	(see *irregardless*)
rest	relax
wrest	take from
retch	vomit
wretch	lowly being, scoundrel
review	survey
revue	a satirical show
right	correct; opposite of *left*
rite	ritual, ceremony
write	to compose letters or words
ring	sound of a bell; jewelry worn around a finger
wring	to twist
road	street, path, highway
rode	past tense of *ride*
rowed	past tense of *row*
roe	fish eggs
row	aisle (pronounced like *oh);* propel with an oar (pronounced like *oh);* fight (pronounced like *wow)*
role	part in a play or film
roll (noun, verb)	a bun; to rotate
roomer	one who rents a room
rumor	innuendo, gossip
root	base of a plant
rout	defeat (pronounced *rowt)*
route	path (pronounced like *root* or *rowt)*
rot	decay, decompose
wrought	accomplished

rote	by memory, formula
wrote	past tense of *write*
rude	impolite, unmannerly
rued	regretted, repented
rye	seed from a grain
wry	mocking, ironic, droll
sacks	large bags
sax	saxophone
saver	one who saves
savor	to appreciate a taste
scene	a view, a setting
seen	to have viewed with eyes
scent	(see *cent*)
sea	a body of salt water
see	to view with eyes
seam	line formed by pieces of fabric sewn together
seem	appear
sear	scorch, burn, or char
seer	one who sees (as in the future)
sere	withered, dry
seas	bodies of salt water
sees	views with eyes
seize	to grab hold of
seed	(see *cede*)
sell	(see *cell*)
semiannual	(see *biannual*)
sensor	(see *censor*)
sent	(see *cent*)
serf	slave
surf (noun, verb)	breaking waves; to ride a surfboard
serial	(see *cereal*)

set	one sets a thing

Example: Please set the table.

sit	one sits oneself

Example: Please sit down at the table.

sew	to stitch
so	in the manner indicated
sow (verb)	to scatter or plant seed

sewer	a conduit for carrying off waste
suer	one who sues

shear	to cut
sheer	transparent

shoe	foot attire
shoo	interjection used to scare away an animal

shoot	(see *chute*)

sic	a Latin term used to indicate that something written is intentionally left in the original form, which may be incorrect.

Example: She wrote, "They made there [sic] beds."

sick	ill

sics	attacks
six	a number

sight	(see *cite*)

sign	an indication
sine	a trigonometry term

since	(see *because*)

sink	to submerge; to descend to a lower level; where you wash dirty dishes
synch (or sync)	to synchronize, to coincide or match up

site	(see *cite*)

slay	kill
sleigh	snow vehicle, sled

sleight	cunning, skill
slight	slender, of little substance
slew	past tense of *slay*
slough	swamp (pronounced *slew* or *slau*)
soar	to fly at great height
sore	in pain
soared	flew at great height
sword	a bladed weapon
sole	bottom of foot; alone
soul	the spiritual part of humans
some	a certain unspecified number
sum	the total from adding numbers
son	male offspring
sun	star that is the central body of the solar system
sonny	diminutive of *son*
sunny	lit or warmed by the sun; cheerful
spade	digging tool
spayed	to have removed the ovaries of an animal
staid	solemn, serious
stayed	remained, waited
stair	step
stare	to look without blinking
stake	a pole
steak	cut of meat
stationary	in one place
stationery	writing paper
steal	rob
steel (noun, adjective)	iron alloy; determined
step (verb, noun)	moving by lifting the foot; degree
steppe	vast grasslands
stile	turnstile, passageway
style	fashion

straight	not curved or bent
strait	narrow passage of water connecting two bodies of water
succor	relief, assistance
sucker	fool
suede	leather finished with a soft, napped surface
swayed	past tense of *sway*; persuaded
suite	a connected series of rooms
sweet	opposite of *sour*
summary	an abstract or brief account
summery	of the summer
sundae	ice cream with syrup
Sunday	day of the week
sympathy	(see *empathy*)
tacks	short nails
tax	percent of earnings paid to the government
tail	hindmost animal appendage
tale	story
take	(see *bring*)
tare	allowance for the weight of packaging
tear (verb)	rip, pull apart
taught	past tense of *teach*
taut	tightly stretched
tea	a beverage
tee	a peg from which a golf ball is hit
team	group playing on the same side in a game
teem	swarm
tear (noun)	salt water coming from eyes when sad (pronounced like *ear*)
tier	a row or layer
tense	nervous strain
tents	portable shelters used for camping

than	used for comparison
then	indicates time, answers *when*
their	possessive pronoun
there	location
they're	contraction for *they are*
threw	past tense of *throw*
through	in one end and out the other
throes	agonizing struggles
throws	tosses, hurls
throne	royal seat or office
thrown	was tossed
thyme	herb of the mint family
time	past, present, future sequences of events
ticks	parasites; sounds of a clock
tics	facial twitches
tide	ebb and flow of the ocean
tied	past tense of *tie*
to	in the direction of, toward
too	also, to an extensive degree

Example: It is too hot to jog.

two	the number after *one*
toad	similar to a frog
toed	having a toe
towed	pulled, hauled
told	said
tolled	sounded a bell
tort	a breach of contract
torte	a rich cake made with little or no flour
tracked	followed
tract	an extended area of land; a political or religious pamphlet
troop	a body of soldiers
troupe	a group of traveling performers

under	(see *fewer*)
vain	excessively concerned about one's appearance
vane	a blade moved by wind as in *weather vane*
vein	blood vessel
vary	to change or alter
very	extremely
verses	lines of poetry
versus	as compared to another choice, against
vial	small container for holding liquids
vile	repulsive, depraved
vice	bad habit; immoral practice
vise	device used to hold an object firmly
wade	to walk through water
weighed	to have put on a scale
wail	mournful cry
whale	marine mammal
waist	narrowest part of the human torso (usually)
waste	to squander or spend uselessly
wait	to be available or ready
weight	quantity of heaviness or mass
waiver	a relinquishment of some right
waver	to feel indecisive; vary
wear	to carry on the body
where	in what place?
warn	to notify
worn	carried on the body; deteriorated
warrantee	person who is given a written guarantee
warranty	written guarantee
way	direction
weigh	to measure mass
we're	contraction for *we are*
were	past tense of *are*

we've	contraction for *we have*
weave	to interlace thread or yarn to make a fabric
weak	lacking strength
week	seven days starting with Sunday
went	(see *gone*)
wheeled	moved on wheels
wield	to exercise power; to handle a weapon effectively
weather	state of the atmosphere in a location
whether	if
which	what one?
witch	sorceress
while	during or in the time that
wile	a trick to fool, trap, or entice
whine	complaining cry
wine	fermented grape juice that becomes an alcoholic beverage
whined	past tense of *whine*, complained
wind	what one does to keep a watch ticking on time (pronounced like *kind*); air current (pronounced like *sinned*)
wined	to supply with wine
whirled	spun rapidly
world	planet Earth
whorled	shaped like a coil
whole	(see *hole*)
wholly	(see *holy*)
who's	contraction for *who is*

Example: Who's at the door?

whose	possessive case of *who*

Example: Whose coat is this?

won	(see *one*)

won't	contraction for *will not*
wont (adjective, noun)	accustomed; habit

wood	tree trunk material
would	expressing an intention

Examples: Would if I could.

wrap	(see *rap)*
wrapped	(see *rapt)*
wreak	(see *reek)*
wrest	(see *rest)*
wretch	(see *retch)*
wring	(see *ring)*
write	(see *right)*
wrote	(see *rote)*
wrought	(see *rot)*
wry	(see *rye)*

yoke	harness for oxen
yolk	yellow center of an egg

yore	long past
you're	contraction for *you are*
your	possessive pronoun

Chapter 3

Punctuation

Spacing with Punctuation

Rule 1. With a typewriter or word processor, you sometimes use one space or two spaces following punctuation. With a computer, use only one space following periods, commas, semicolons, colons, exclamation points, question marks, and quotation marks. With a computer, the space needed after these punctuation marks is proportioned automatically.

Rule 2. Use no spaces on either side of a hyphen. (For more rules about hyphens, see page 65).

Example: We borrowed twenty-three sheets of paper.

Note

For spacing with ellipsis marks, see the section that follows. For spacing with *en* and *em* dashes, see page 68.

Periods

Rule 1. Use a period at the end of a complete sentence that is a statement.

Example: I know that you would never break my trust intentionally.

Rule 2. If the last word in the sentence ends in a period, do not follow it with another period.

Examples: I know that M.D. She is my sister-in-law.
Please shop, cook, etc. I will do the laundry.

Rule 3. Use a period after an indirect question.

> *Example:* *He asked where his suitcase was.*

Ellipsis Marks

Use ellipsis marks when omitting a word, phrase, line, paragraph, or more from a quoted passage.

Note

To create ellipsis marks with a PC, type the period three times and the spacing will be automatically set, or press Ctrl-Alt and the period once.

The Three-dot Method

There are many methods for using ellipses. The three-dot method is the simplest and is appropriate for most general works and many scholarly ones. The three- or four-dot method and an even more rigorous method used in legal works require fuller explanations that can be found in other reference books.

Rule 1. Use no more than three marks whether the omission occurs in the middle of a sentence or between sentences.

> *Example:* Original sentence: *The regulation states, "All agencies must document overtime or risk losing federal funds."*
> Rewritten using ellipses: *The regulation states, "All agencies must document overtime..."*

Note

With the three-dot method, you may leave out punctuation such as commas that were in the original.

> *Example:* Original sentence from Lincoln's Gettysburg Address:
> *"Four score and seven years ago our fathers brought forth, upon this continent, a new nation, conceived in liberty, and dedicated to the proposition that all men are created equal."*
> Rewritten using ellipses: *" Four score and seven years ago our fathers brought forth... a new nation, conceived in liberty..."*

Rule 2. When you omit one or more paragraphs within a long quotation, use ellipsis marks after the last punctuation mark that ends the preceding paragraph.

Commas

Rule 1. To avoid confusion, use commas to separate words and word groups with a series of three or more.

> *Example: My $10 million estate is to be split among my husband, daughter, son, and nephew.*

Omitting the comma after son would indicate that the son and nephew would have to split one-third of the estate.

Rule 2. Use a comma to separate two adjectives when the word *and* can be inserted between them.

> *Examples: He is a strong, healthy man.*
> *We stayed at an expensive summer resort.* You would not say *expensive and summer resort,* so no comma.

Rule 3. Use a comma when an *-ly* adjective is used with other adjectives.

Note

To test whether an *-ly* word is an adjective, see if it can be used alone with the noun. If it can, use the comma.

> *Examples: Felix was a lonely, young boy.*
> *I get headaches in brightly lit rooms. Brightly* is not an adjective because it cannot be used alone with *rooms*; therefore, no comma is used between *brightly* and *lit.*

Rule 4. Use commas before or surrounding the name or title of a person directly addressed.

> *Examples: Will you, Aisha, do that assignment for me?*
> *Yes, Doctor, I will.*

Note

Capitalize a title when directly addressing someone.

Rule 5a. Use a comma to separate the day of the month from the year and after the year.

> *Example: Kathleen met her husband on December 5, 2003, in Mill Valley, California.*

Rule 5b. If any part of the date is omitted, leave out the comma.
Example: They met in December 2003 in Mill Valley.

Rule 6. Use a comma to separate the city from the state and after the state. Some businesses no longer use the comma after the state.

Example: I lived in San Francisco, California, for twenty years.

OR

I lived in San Francisco, California for twenty years.

Rule 7. Use commas to surround degrees or titles used with names. Commas are no longer required around *Jr.* and *Sr.* Commas never set off *II, III,* and so forth.

Example: Al Mooney, M.D., knew Sam Sunny Jr. and Charles Starr III.

Rule 8. Use commas to set off expressions that interrupt the flow of the sentence.

Example: I am, as you have probably noticed, very nervous about this.

Rule 9. When starting a sentence with a weak clause, use a comma after it. Conversely, do not use a comma when the sentence starts with a strong clause followed by a weak clause.

Examples: If you are not sure about this, let me know now.
Let me know now if you are not sure about this.

Rule 10. Use a comma after phrases of more than three words that begin a sentence. If the phrase has fewer than three words, the comma is optional.

Examples: To apply for this job, you must have previous experience.
On February 14 many couples give each other candy or flowers.
OR
On February 14, many couples give each other candy or flowers.

Rule 11. If something or someone is sufficiently identified, the description following it is considered nonessential and should be surrounded by commas.

Examples: Freddy, who has a limp, was in an auto accident. Freddy is named, so the description is not essential.
The boy who has a limp was in an auto accident. We do not know which boy is being referred to without further description; therefore, no commas are used.

Rule 12. Use a comma to separate two strong clauses joined by a coordinating conjunction—*and, or, but, for, nor*. You can omit the comma if the clauses are both short.

> *Examples: I have painted the entire house, but he is still working on sanding the doors.*
> *I paint and he writes.*

Rule 13. Use the comma to separate two sentences if it will help avoid confusion.

> *Example: I chose the colors red and green, and blue was his first choice.*

Rule 14. A **comma splice** is an error caused by joining two strong clauses with only a comma instead of separating the clauses with a conjunction, a semicolon, or a period. A **run-on sentence**, which is incorrect, is created by joining two strong clauses without any punctuation.

> *Incorrect: Time flies when we are having fun, we are always having fun.*
> (Comma splice)
> *Incorrect: Time flies when we are having fun we are always having fun.*
> (Run-on sentence)
> *Correct: Time flies when we are having fun; we are always having fun.*
> **OR**
> *Time flies when we are having fun, and we are always having fun.*
> (Comma is optional because both strong clauses are short.)
> **OR**
> *Time flies when we are having fun. We are always having fun.*

Rule 15. If the subject does not appear in front of the second verb, do not use a comma.

> *Example: He thought quickly but still did not answer correctly.*

Rule 16. Use commas to introduce or interrupt direct quotations shorter than three lines.

> *Examples: He actually said, "I do not care."*
> *"Why," I asked, "do you always forget to do it?"*

Rule 17. Use a comma to separate a statement from a question.

> *Example: I can go, can't I?*

Rule 18. Use a comma to separate contrasting parts of a sentence.

Example: That is my money, not yours.

Rule 19. Use a comma when beginning sentences with introductory words such as *well, now*, or *yes*.

Examples: Yes, I do need that report.
Well, I never thought I'd live to see the day . . .

Rule 20. Use commas surrounding words such as *therefore* and *however* when they are used as interrupters.

Examples: I would, therefore, like a response.
I would be happy, however, to volunteer for the Red Cross.

Rule 21. Use either a comma or a semicolon before introductory words such as *namely, that is, i.e., for example, e.g.,* or *for instance* when they are followed by a series of items. Use a comma after the introductory word.

Examples: You may be required to bring many items, e.g., sleeping bags,
pans, and warm clothing.

   OR

You may be required to bring many items; e.g., sleeping bags,
pans, and warm clothing.
You may be required to bring many items, e.g. sleeping bags,
pans, and warm clothing.

Note

i.e. means *that is; e.g.* means *for example.*

Semicolons

Rule 1. Use a semicolon in place of a period to separate two sentences where the conjunction has been left out.

Examples: Call me tomorrow; I will give you my answer then.
I have paid my dues; therefore, I expect all the privileges listed
in the contract.

Rule 2. It is preferable to use the semicolon before introductory words such as *namely, however, therefore, that is, i.e., for example, e.g.,* or *for instance* when they introduce a complete sentence. It is also preferable to use a comma after the introductory word.

> *Examples:* *You will want to bring many backpacking items; for example, sleeping bags, pans, and warm clothing will make the trip better.*
>
> *As we discussed, you will bring two items; i.e., a sleeping bag and a tent are not optional.*

Rule 3. Use either a semicolon or a comma before introductory words such as *namely, however, therefore, that is, i.e., for example, e.g.,* or *for instance* when they introduce a list following a complete sentence. Use a comma after the introductory word.

> *Example:* *You will want to bring many backpacking items; for example, sleeping bags, pans, and warm clothing.*
>
> **OR**
>
> *Example:* *You will want to bring many backpacking items, for example, sleeping bags, pans, and warm clothing.*

Rule 4. Use the semicolon to separate units of a series when one or more of the units contain commas.

> *Example:* *This conference has people who have come from Boise, Idaho; Los Angeles, California; and Nashville, Tennessee.*

Rule 5. Use the semicolon between two sentences that are joined by a conjunction but already have one or more commas within the first sentence.

> *Examples:* *When I finish here, I will be glad to help you; and that is a promise I will keep.*
>
> *If she can, she will attempt that feat; and if her husband is able, he will be there to see her.*

Colons

Rule 1. Use the colon after a complete sentence to introduce a list of items when introductory words such as *namely, for example,* or *that is* do not appear.

> *Examples:* *You may be required to bring many items: sleeping bags, pans, and warm clothing.*
>
> *I want the following items: butter, sugar, and flour.*
>
> *I want an assistant who can do the following: (1) input data, (2) write reports, and (3) complete tax forms.*

Rule 2. A colon should not precede a list unless it follows a complete sentence; however, the colon is a style choice that some publications allow.

Examples: If a waitress wants to make a good impression on her customers and boss, she should (a) dress appropriately, (b) calculate the bill carefully, and (c) be courteous to customers.

There are three ways a waitress can make a good impression on her boss and her customers:

(a) *Dress appropriately.*

(b) *Calculate the bill carefully.*

(c) *Be courteous to customers.*

I want an assistant who can (1) input data, (2) write reports, and (3) complete tax forms.

Rule 3. Capitalization and punctuation are optional when using single words or phrases in bulleted form. If each bullet or numbered point is a complete sentence, capitalize the first word and end each sentence with proper ending punctuation. The rule of thumb is to be consistent.

Examples: I want an assistant who can do the following:

(a) *input data,*

(b) *write reports, and*

(c) *complete tax forms.*

The following are requested:

(a) *Wool sweaters for possible cold weather.*

(b) *Wet suits for snorkeling.*

(c) *Introductions to the local dignitaries.*

OR

The following are requested:

(a) *wool sweaters for possible cold weather*

(b) *wet suits for snorkeling*

(c) *introductions to the local dignitaries*

Note

With lists, you may use periods after numbers and letters instead of parentheses.

These are some of the pool rules:

1. *Do not run.*
2. *If you see unsafe behavior, report it to the lifeguard.*
3. *Have fun!*

Rule 4. Use a colon instead of a semicolon between two strong clauses (sentences) when the second clause explains or illustrates the first clause and no coordinating conjunction is being used to connect the clauses. If only one sentence follows the colon, do not capitalize the first word of the new sentence. If two or more sentences follow the colon, capitalize the first word of each sentence following.

> **Examples:** *I enjoy reading: novels by Kurt Vonnegut are among my favorites.*
> *Garlic is used in Italian cooking: It greatly enhances the flavor of pasta dishes. It also enhances the flavor of eggplant.*

Rule 5. Use the colon to introduce a direct quotation that is more than three lines in length. In this situation, leave a blank line above and below the quoted material. Single space the long quotation. Some style manuals say to indent one-half inch on both the left and right margins; others say to indent only on the left margin. Quotation marks are not used.

> **Example:**
>
> *The author of <u>Touched,</u> Jane Straus, wrote in the first chapter:*
>
> *Georgia went back to her bed and stared at the intricate patterns of burned moth wings in the translucent glass of the overhead light. Her father was in "hyper mode" again where nothing could calm him down.*
>
> *He'd been talking nonstop for a week about remodeling projects, following her around the house as she tried to escape his chatter. He was just about to crash, she knew.*

Rule 6. Use the colon to follow the salutation of a business letter even when addressing someone by his/her first name. Never use a semicolon after a salutation. A comma is used after the salutation for personal correspondence.

> **Example:** *Dear Ms. Rodriguez:*

Question Marks

> **Rule 1**. Use a question mark only after a direct question.
>
> > **Examples:** *Will you go with me?*
> > *I asked if he would go with me.*

Rule 2. Use a question mark when a sentence is half statement and half question.

Example: You do care, don't you?

Exclamation Points

Rule. Use exclamation points to show emphasis or surprise. Do not use the exclamation point in formal business letters.

Example: I'm truly shocked by your behavior!

Quotation Marks

Rule 1. Periods and commas always go inside quotation marks, even inside single quotes.

Examples: The sign changed from "Walk," to "Don't Walk," to "Walk"
    again within thirty seconds.
    She said, "Hurry up."
    She said, "He said, 'Hurry up.'"

Rule 2. The placement of question marks with quotes follows logic. If a question is in quotation marks, the question mark should be placed inside the quotation marks.

Examples: She asked, "Will you still be my friend?"
    Do you agree with the saying, "All's fair in love and war"?
    Here the question is outside the quote.

Note

Only one ending punctuation mark is used with quotation marks. Also, the stronger punctuation mark wins. Therefore, no period after *war* is used.

Rule 3. When you have a question outside quoted material AND inside quoted material, use only one question mark and place it inside the quotation mark.

Example: Did she say, "May I go?"

Rule 4. Use single quotation marks for quotes within quotes. Note that the period goes inside all quote marks.

Example: He said, "Danea said, 'Do not treat me that way.'"

Rule 5. Use quotation marks to set off a direct quotation only.

Examples: "When will you be here?" he asked.
He asked when you will be there.

Rule 6. Do not use quotation marks with quoted material that is more than three lines in length. See Colons, Rule 5, p. 60 for style guidance with longer quotes.

Rule 7. When you are quoting something that has a spelling or grammar mistake or presents material in a confusing way, insert the term *sic* in italics and enclose it in brackets. *Sic* means, "This is the way the original material was."

Example: She wrote, "I would rather die then [sic] be seen wearing the
same outfit as my sister."
*Should be *than*, not *then*.*

Parentheses

Rule 1. Use parentheses to enclose words or figures that clarify or are used as an aside.

Examples: I expect five hundred dollars ($500).
He finally answered (after taking five minutes to think) that he
did not understand the question.

Commas could have been used in the above example. Parentheses show less emphasis or importance. Em dashes (see page 69), which could also have been used instead of parentheses, show emphasis.

Rule 2. Use full parentheses to enclose numbers or letters used for listed items.

Example: We need an emergency room physician who can (1) think
quickly, (2) treat patients respectfully, and (3) handle
complaints from the public.

Rule 3. Periods go inside parentheses only if an entire sentence is inside the parentheses.

Examples: Please read the analysis (I enclosed it as Attachment A.).
OR
Please read the analysis. (I enclosed it as Attachment A.)
OR
Please read the analysis (Attachment A).

Apostrophes

Rule 1. Use the apostrophe with contractions. The apostrophe is always placed at the spot where the letter(s) has been removed.

   Examples: *don't, isn't*

   You're right.

   She's a great teacher.

Rule 2. Use the apostrophe to show possession. Place the apostrophe before the *s* to show singular possession.

   Examples: *one boy's hat*

   one woman's hat

   one actress's hat

   one child's hat

   Ms. Chang's house

Note

Although names ending in *s* or an *s* sound are not required to have the second *s* added in possessive form, it is preferred.

   Mr. Jones's golf clubs
   Texas's weather
   Ms. Straus's daughter
   Jose Sanchez's artwork
   Dr. Hastings's appointment (name is *Hastings*)
   Mrs. Lees's books (name is *Lees*)

Rule 3. Use the apostrophe where the noun that should follow is implied.

   Example: *This was his father's, not his, jacket.*

Rule 4. To show plural possession, make the noun plural first. Then immediately use the apostrophe.

   Examples: *two boys' hats*

   two women's hats

   two actresses' hats

   two children's hats

   the Changs' house

   the Joneses' golf clubs

   the Strauses' daughter

   the Sanchezes' artwork

the Hastingses' appointment
the Leeses' books

Rule 5. Do not use an apostrophe for the plural of a name.

Examples: We visited the Sanchezes in Los Angeles.
The Changs have two cats and a dog.

Rule 6. With a singular compound noun, show possession with *'s* at the end of the word.

Example: my mother-in-law's hat

Rule 7. If the compound noun is plural, form the plural first and then use the apostrophe.

Example: my two brothers-in-law's hats

Rule 8. Use the apostrophe and *s* after the second name only if two people possess the same item.

Examples: Cesar and Maribel's home is constructed of redwood.
Cesar's and Maribel's job contracts will be renewed next year.
There is separate ownership.

Cesar and Maribel's job contracts will be renewed next year.
There is joint ownership of more than one contract.

Rule 9. Never use an apostrophe with possessive pronouns: *his, hers, its, theirs, ours, yours, whose.* They already show possession so they do not require an apostrophe.

Examples:
Correct: *This book is hers, not yours.*
Incorrect: *Sincerely your's.*

Rule 10. The only time an apostrophe is used for *it's* is when it is a contraction for *it is* or *it has.*

Examples: It's a nice day.
It's your right to refuse the invitation.
It's been great getting to know you.

Rule 11. The plurals for capital letters and numbers used as nouns are not formed with apostrophes.

Examples: She consulted with three M.D.s.
BUT
She went to three M.D.s' offices.

The apostrophe is needed here to show plural possessive.

She learned her ABCs.
*the 1990s, **not** the 1990's*
*the '90s or the mid-'70s, **not** the '90's or the mid-'70's*
She learned her times tables for 6s and 7s.

Exception: Use apostrophes with capital letters and numbers when the meaning would be unclear otherwise.

Examples: Please dot your I's.
You don't mean Is.
Ted couldn't distinguish between her 6's and 0's.
You don't mean Os.

<u>Rule 12</u>. Use the possessive case in front of a gerund (-*ing* word).

Examples: Alex's skating was a joy to behold.
This does not stop Joan's inspecting of our facilities next Thursday.

<u>Rule 13</u>. If the gerund has a pronoun in front of it, use the possessive form of that pronoun.

Examples: I appreciate your inviting me to dinner.
I appreciated his working with me to resolve the conflict.

Hyphens

Hyphens Between Words

<u>Rule 1</u>. To check whether a compound noun is two words, one word, or hyphenated, you may need to look it up in the dictionary. If you can't find the word in the dictionary, treat the noun as separate words.

Examples: eyewitness
eye shadow
eye-opener

Note

All these words had to be looked up in the dictionary to know what to do with them!

Rule 2. Phrases that have verb, noun, and adjective forms should appear as separate words when used as verbs and as one word when used as nouns or adjectives.

> *Examples: The engine will eventually **break down**. (verb)*
> *We suffered a **breakdown** in communications. (noun)*
> *Please **clean up** your room. (verb)*
> *That Superfund site will require specialized **cleanup** procedures. (adjective)*

Rule 3. Compound verbs are either hyphenated or appear as one word. If you do not find the verb in the dictionary, hyphenate it.

> *Examples: To **air-condition** the house will be costly.*
> *We were notified that management will **downsize** the organization next year.*

Rule 4. Generally, hyphenate between two or more adjectives when they come before a noun and act as a single idea.

> *Examples: friendly-looking man*
> (compound adjective in front of a noun)
> *friendly little girl*
> (not a compound adjective)
> *brightly lit room*
> (*Brightly* is an adverb describing *lit*, not an adjective.)

Rule 5. When adverbs other than -*ly* adverbs are used as compound words in front of a noun, hyphenate. When the combination of words is used after the noun, do not hyphenate.

> *Examples: The **well-known** actress accepted her award.*
>
> *Well* is an adverb followed by another descriptive word. They combine to form one idea in front of the noun.
>
> *The actress who accepted her award was **well known**.*
> *Well known* follows the noun it describes, so no hyphen is used.
>
> *A **long-anticipated** decision was finally made.*
>
> *He got a **much-needed** haircut yesterday.*
>
> *His haircut was **much needed**.*

Rule 6. Remember to use a comma, not a hyphen, between two adjectives when you could have used *and* between them.

Examples: I have important, classified documents.
Jennifer received a lovely, fragrant bouquet on Valentine's Day.

Rule 7. Hyphenate all compound numbers from *twenty-one* through *ninety-nine*.

Examples: The teacher had thirty-two children in her classroom.
Only twenty-one of the children were bilingual.

Rule 8. Hyphenate all spelled-out fractions.

Examples: You need one-third of a cup of sugar for that recipe.
More than one-half of the student body voted for removing soda machines from campus.

Hyphens with Prefixes

Rule 1. The current trend is to do away with unnecessary hyphens. Therefore, attach most prefixes and suffixes onto root words without a hyphen.

Examples: noncompliance
copayment
semiconscious
fortyish

Rule 2. Hyphenate prefixes when they come before proper nouns.

Example: un-American

Rule 3. Hyphenate prefixes ending in an *a* or *i* only when the root word begins with the same letter.

Examples: ultra-ambitious
semi-invalid

Rule 4. When a prefix ends in one vowel and a root word begins with a different vowel, generally attach them without a hyphen.

Examples: antiaircraft
proactive

Rule 5. Prefixes and root words that result in double *e*'s and double *o*'s are usually combined to form one word.

Examples: preemployment
coordinate
Exceptions: de-emphasize
co-owner

Rule 6. Hyphenate all words beginning with *self* except for *selfish* and *selfless*.

>   *Examples: self-assured*
>   *self-respect*
>   *self-addressed*

Rule 7. Use a hyphen with the prefix *ex*.

>   *Example: His ex-wife sued for nonsupport.*

Rule 8. Use the hyphen with the prefix *re* only when:

>   the *re-* means *again* AND omitting the hyphen would
>   cause confusion with another word.

>   *Examples: Will she recover from her illness?*
>   *Re-* does not mean *again.*
>   *I have re-covered the sofa twice.*
>   *Re-* does mean *again* AND omitting the hyphen would
>   have caused confusion with another word.
>   *The stamps have been reissued.*
>   *Re-* means *again* but would not cause confusion with
>   another word.
>   *I must re-press the shirt.*
>   *Re* means *again* AND omitting the hyphen would have
>   caused confusion with another word.

Dashes

En Dash

An **en dash,** which is a little longer than a hyphen, is used for periods of time when you might otherwise use *to.*

>   *Examples: The years 2001–2003 [This is how the spacing would appear on a*
>   *PC.]*
>   *January–June   [On a Mac, use no spaces or only small spaces*
>   *surrounding the en dash.]*

An **en dash** is also used in place of a hyphen when combining open compounds.

>   *Examples: North Carolina–Virginia border*
>   *a high school–college conference*

With an **en dash**, spacing is dependent on your computer. If you are forming an **en dash** using a PC, hit the space bar, then the Hyphen key, and then hit the space bar again before typing in the next word/number.

If you are using a Mac, press the Option key and the Hyphen key to form an **en dash**.

Em Dash

Use an **em dash** sparingly in formal writing. Don't use it just because you are uncertain about correct punctuation. In informal writing, **em dashes** may replace commas, semicolons, colons, and parentheses to indicate added emphasis, an interruption, or an abrupt change of thought.

On a PC, an **em dash** is made by typing two hyphens with no spaces before or after. It looks like this:—

On a Mac, an **em dash** is made by striking Option-Shift-Hyphen.

Examples: *You are the friend—the only friend—who offered to help me.*
Never have I met such a lovely person—before you.
I pay the bills—she has all the fun.
A semicolon would be used here in formal writing.

I need three items at the store—dog food, vegetarian chili, and cheddar cheese.
Remember, a colon would be used here in formal writing.
My agreement with Fiona is clear—she teaches me French and I teach her German.
Again, a colon would work here in formal writing.

Please call my agent—Jessica Cohen—about hiring me.
Parentheses or commas would work just fine here instead of the dashes.

I wish you would—oh, never mind.
This shows an abrupt change in thought and warrants an **em dash**.

While there are many more possible uses of the **em dash**, by not providing additional rules, I am hoping to curb your temptation to employ this convenient but overused punctuation mark.

Chapter 4
Capitalization

Rule 1. Capitalize the first word of a quoted sentence.

> *Examples: He said, "Treat her as you would your own daughter."*
> *"Look out!" she screamed. "You almost ran into my child."*

Rule 2. Capitalize a proper noun.

> *Example: Golden Gate Bridge*

Rule 3. Capitalize a person's title when it precedes the name. Do not capitalize when the title is acting as a description following the name.

> *Examples: Chairperson Petrov*
> *Ms. Petrov, the chairperson of the company, will address us at noon.*

Rule 4. Capitalize the person's title when it follows the name on the address or signature line.

> *Example: Sincerely,*
> *Ms. Haines, Chairperson*

Rule 5. Capitalize the titles of high-ranking government officials when used with or before their names. Do not capitalize the civil title if it is used instead of the name.

> *Examples: The president will address Congress.*
> *All senators are expected to attend.*
> *The governors, lieutenant governors, and attorneys general called for a special task force.*
> *Governor Fortinbrass, Lieutenant Governor Poppins, Attorney General Dalloway, and Senators James and Twain will attend.*

Rule 6. Capitalize any title when used as a direct address.

> *Example: Will you take my temperature, Doctor?*

Rule 7. Capitalize points of the compass only when they refer to specific regions.

> *Examples: We have had three relatives visit from the South.*
> *Go south three blocks and then turn left.*
> *We live in the southeast section of town.*
> *Southeast is just an adjective here describing section, so it should not be capitalized.*

Rule 8. Always capitalize the first and last words of titles of publications regardless of their parts of speech. Capitalize other words within titles, including the short verb forms *Is, Are*, and *Be*.

> *Exception: Do not capitalize little words within titles such as a, an, the, but, as, if, and, or, nor or prepositions, regardless of their length.*
> *Examples: The Day of the Jackal*
> *What Color Is Your Parachute?*
> *A Tale of Two Cities*

Rule 9. Capitalize *federal* or *state* when used as part of an official agency name or in government documents where these terms represent an official name. If they are being used as general terms, you may use lowercase letters.

> *Examples: The state has evidence to the contrary.*
> *That is a federal offense.*
> *The State Board of Equalization collects sales taxes.*
> *We will visit three states during our summer vacation.*
> *The Federal Bureau of Investigation has been subject to much scrutiny and criticism lately.*
> *Her business must comply with all county, state, and federal laws.*

Rule 10. You may capitalize words such as *department, bureau*, and *office* if you have prepared your text in the following way:

> *Example: The Bureau of Land Management (Bureau) has some jurisdiction over Indian lands. The Bureau is finding its administrative role to be challenging.*

Rule 11. Do not capitalize names of seasons.

Example: I love autumn colors and spring flowers.

Rule 12. Capitalize the first word of a salutation and the first word of a complimentary close.

Examples: Dear Ms. Mohamed:
My dear Mr. Sanchez:
Very truly yours,

Rule 13. Capitalize words derived from proper nouns.

Example: I must take English and math.
English is capitalized because it comes from the proper noun *England,* but *math* does not come from *mathland.*

Rule 14. Capitalize the names of specific course titles.

Example: I must take history and Algebra 2.

Rule 15. After a sentence ending with a colon, do not capitalize the first word if it begins a list.

Example: These are my favorite foods: chocolate cake, spaghetti, and artichokes.

Rule 16. Do not capitalize when only one sentence follows a sentence ending with a colon.

Example: I love Jane Smiley's writing: her book, A Thousand Acres, *was beautiful.*

Rule 17. Capitalize when two or more sentences follow a sentence ending with a colon.

Example: I love Jane Smiley's writing: Her book, A Thousand Acres, *was beautiful. Also,* Moo *was clever.*

Chapter 5

Writing Numbers

Rule 1. Some authorities say that the numbers *one* through *nine* or *ten* should be spelled out and figures used for higher numbers. Other authorities spell out *one* through *one hundred*, plus even hundreds, thousands, and so on. The best strategy is to be consistent.

> *Correct Examples:* I want five copies, not ten copies.
> I want 5 copies, not 10 copies.

Rule 2. Be consistent within a category. For example, if you choose numerals because one of the numbers you must deal with is greater than *ten*, you should use numerals for everything in that category.

> *Correct Examples:* Given the budget constraints, if all 30 history students attend the four plays, then the 7 math students will be able to attend only two plays.
> (*Students* are represented with figures; *plays* are represented with words.)
> My 10 cats fought with their 2 cats.
> My ten cats fought with their two cats.

> *Incorrect Example:* I asked for five pencils, not 50.

Rule 3. Always spell out simple fractions and use hyphens with them.

> *Examples:* One-half of the pies have been eaten.
> A two-thirds majority is required for that bill to pass in Congress.

Rule 4. A mixed fraction can be expressed in figures unless it is the first word of a sentence.

> *Examples:* We expect a $5\frac{1}{2}$ percent wage increase.
> Five and one-half percent was the maximum allowable interest.

Rule 5. The simplest way to express large numbers is best. Round numbers are usually spelled out. Be careful to be consistent within a sentence.

> *Correct:*   *You can earn from one million to five million dollars.*
> *Incorrect: You can earn from one million to $5,000,000.*
> *Correct:*   *You can earn from five hundred to five million dollars.*
> *Correct*:   *You can earn from $5 hundred to $5 million.*
> *Incorrect: You can earn from $500 to $5 million.*
> *Incorrect: You can earn from $500 to five million dollars.*

Rule 6. Write decimals in figures. Put a zero in front of a decimal unless the decimal itself begins with a zero.

> *Examples: The plant grew 0.79 of a foot in one year.*
> *The plant grew only .07 of a foot this year because of the drought.*

Rule 7. When writing out large numbers of five or more digits before the decimal point, use a comma where the comma would appear in the figure format. Use the word *and* only where the decimal point appears in the figure format.

> *Examples: $15,768.13: Fifteen thousand, seven hundred sixty-eight dollars and thirteen cents*
> *$1054.21: One thousand fifty-four dollars and twenty-one cents*

Note

The comma is now commonly omitted in four-digit whole numbers.

Rule 8. The following examples apply when using dates:

> *Examples: The meeting is scheduled for June 30.*
> *The meeting is scheduled for the 30th of June.*
> *We have had tricks played on us on April 1.*
> *The 1st of April puts some people on edge.*

Rule 9. When expressing decades, you may spell them out and lowercase them.

> *Example: During the eighties and nineties, the U.S. economy grew.*

Rule 10. If you wish to express decades using incomplete numerals, put an apostrophe before the incomplete numeral but not between the year and the *s*.

>   ***Correct:***   *During the '80s and '90s, the U.S. economy grew.*
>   ***Incorrect:*** *During the '80's and '90's, the U.S. economy grew.*

Rule 11. You may also express decades in complete numerals. Again, don't use an apostrophe between the year and the *s*.

>   ***Example:*** *During the 1980s and 1990s, the U.S. economy grew.*

Rule 12. Normally, spell out the time of day in text even with half and quarter hours. With *o'clock*, the number is always spelled out.

>   ***Examples:*** *She gets up at four thirty before the baby wakes up.*
>   *The baby wakes up at five o'clock in the morning.*

Rule 13. Use numerals with the time of day when exact times are being emphasized or when using A.M. or P.M.

>   ***Examples:*** *Monib's flight leaves at 6:22 A.M.*
>   *Please arrive by 12:30 sharp.*
>   *She had a 7:00 P.M. deadline.*

Rule 14. Use *noon* and *midnight* rather than *12:00 A.M.* or *12:00 P.M.*

Rule 15. Hyphenate all compound numbers from *twenty-one* through *ninety-nine*.

>   ***Example:*** *Forty-three people were injured in the train wreck.*
>   *Twenty-three of them were hospitalized.*

Rule 16. Write out a number if it begins a sentence.

>   ***Examples:*** *Twenty-nine people won an award for helping their*
>   *communities.*
>   *That 29 people won an award for helping their communities*
>   *was fantastic!* OR
>   *That twenty-nine people won an award for helping their*
>   *communities was fantastic!*

Chapter 6

Quizzes

Grammar Pretest

Correct the grammar error in each sentence. The answers are on page 116.

> **Example:** *Shoshana felt badly about failing the Geometry test.*
> **Correction:** *Shoshana felt bad about failing the Geometry test.*

1. How quick he runs.
2. Neither DeAndre nor I are to follow.
3. The desk and the chair sits in the corner.
4. Each of us were scheduled to take the test.
5. The coach, not the players, have been ill.
6. There is only four days until Christmas.
7. She is one of the women who works hard.
8. That was Yusuf and me whom you saw.
9. This phone call is for Bill and I.
10. Terrell is the smartest of the two.
11. It was I whom called.
12. It is us clerks who work hard.
13. He took the plate off of the table.
14. None of the neighbors offered his support.
15. They mailed the copies to him and I.

16. Neither of the candidates have spoken.

17. How will you be effected financially if the effect of downsizing means you will lose your job?

18. Joan walks slower so her children can keep up with her.

19. Jake is the oldest of the two brothers.

20. May did good on the test she took yesterday.

21. He and she were real close friends.

22. Whomever drove in the carpool lane without any passengers will be fined.

23. Please allow Jenna or myself to assist you.

24. I work with people that judge others by their nationalities and accents.

25. They fought over their father's estate because they felt angrily about the way he had treated them.

26. You look well in that running outfit.

27. Don't feel badly about forgetting my birthday.

28. We saw two puppies at the pound and took home the cutest one.

29. Speak slower please.

30. Samantha will meet us later on.

31. Pollen effects my sinuses and makes me sneeze.

32. I want to lay down for a nap, but the phone keeps ringing.

33. That SUV, that landed on its hood after the accident, was traveling at eighty miles per hour.

34. Yesterday, Barry lay my jacket on the hood of the car.

35. How much further before we arrive in Santa Fe?

36. My daughter became a honorary member of the city council for the day.

37. In the end, we had to decide among a minivan and a station wagon as our second car.

38. Your the only one for me.

39. That redwood tree has become taller then the oak tree next door.

40. The time for action has long since past.

41. Its a long way from here to Tierra del Fuego.

42. Mother, can I go to the movies with Ashton this afternoon?

43. I could of danced all night.

44. Srdjian immigrated from his native Bosnia about five years ago.

45. I am tiring of the noise from the continual flow of traffic past my apartment.

46. The teacher tried to illicit a discussion about the novel.

47. La Donna talks fondly about the four years that she has went to the university.

48. The answer is plane and simple.

49. Let me sit this book down on the table before I answer your question.

50. The legislature finally authorized the funds to polish the gold on the dome of the capital building.

Finding Subjects and Verbs **Quiz 1**

Underline the subjects once and the verbs twice. Answers are on page 118.

Example: She scratched her silver ring against the edge of the pool.

1. He depends on her in times of need.

2. Watch your step.

3. The insurance agent gave her sound advice.

4. On the table was her purse.

5. In the newspaper, an interesting article appeared.

6. Look before you leap.

7. Across the road lived her boyfriend.

8. We are forced to inhale and exhale this smog-filled air.

9. In the gutter, I found a shiny new dime.

10. Around every cloud is a silver lining.

11. Every one of the roses bloomed.

Finding Subjects and Verbs **Quiz 2**

Underline the verbs twice and the subjects once. Answers are on page 118.

Example: Have you considered running for public office?

1. This gorgeous grand piano is tuned to perfection.

2. Every environmental regulation has been undermined by that industry.

3. My gift for walking and talking simultaneously did not go unnoticed.

4. Your red <u>scarf</u> <u>matches</u> your eyes.

5. Every <u>attempt</u> to flatter him <u>failed</u> miserably.

6. <u>Think</u> before <u>you</u> <u>speak</u> and <u>you</u> <u>will</u> <u>be</u> glad for the things <u>you</u> never <u>said</u>.

7. If <u>all</u> <u>is</u> lost, why <u>am</u> <u>I</u> still <u>playing</u>?

8. <u>Jared</u> <u>needed</u> a pity party after he <u>lost</u> his job.

9. <u>Have</u> <u>you</u> <u>memorized</u> all the chemical symbols on the chart?

10. *<u>Buses</u>* <u>has</u> only one *s* in the middle of it.

✗ 11. Please <u>answer</u> the question without smirking.

Subject and Verb Agreement <u>Quiz 1</u>

Underline the verbs twice and the subjects once. If the subjects and verbs do not agree, change the verbs to match the subjects. Answers are on page 119. Place a check mark in front of sentences that are correct.

Example: *The <u>box</u> of books <u>were opened</u> yesterday.*
Correction: *The <u>box</u> of books <u>was opened</u> yesterday.*

1. At the end of the story, they ~~was~~ were <u>living</u> happily ever after.

2. <u>Al</u> and <u>Eli</u> <u>go</u> to the beach to surf with their friends.

3. When <u>Al</u> and <u>Eli</u> <u>arrive</u>, they <u>find</u> that their <u>friends</u> ~~has~~ have <u>waxed</u> their boards.

4. The <u>group</u> of children from that school <u>has</u> never <u>seen</u> the ocean.

5. If our <u>staff members</u> don't <u>quit</u> picking at each other, <u>we</u> <u>will</u> not <u>meet</u> our goals.

6. Either <u>Gary</u> or <u>I</u> ~~are~~ am <u>responsible</u> for allocating the funds.

7. Neither <u>she</u> nor <u>they</u> <u>were</u> willing to predict the election results.

8. <u>Nora</u> <u>is</u> one of the candidates who <u>is</u> worthy of my vote.

9. Nora, of all the candidates who is running, is the best.

10. My problem, which is minor in comparison with others, exist because I dropped out of high school.

11. His dogs, which are kept outside, bark all day long.

12. There's three strawberries left.

13. Here is the reports from yesterday.

14. Some of my goals has yet to be met.

15. All of my goals are being met and surpassed.

16. None of this is your business.

17. None of them is coming home tonight.

18. One-third of the city are experiencing a blackout tonight.

19. One-third of the people are suffering.

20. When she talks, we listens.

21. Neither the farmer nor the farm workers is willing to settle the strike.

22. Neither Darren nor Ida are capable of such a crime.

Subject and Verb Agreement <u>Quiz 2</u>

Underline the verbs twice and the subjects once. If the subjects and verbs do not agree, change the verbs to match the subjects. Place a check mark in front of sentences that are correct. The answers are on page 120.

> *Example:*   *The <u>supervisor</u> or <u>the employees</u> <u>is</u> <u>holding</u> a press conference.*
> *Correction: The <u>supervisor</u> or <u>the employees</u> <u>are</u> <u>holding</u> a press conference.*

1. The teacher or student is going to appear on stage first.

2. The mother duck, along with all her ducklings, swim so gracefully.

3. Each of those dresses is beautiful.

4. The folder, not the letters, were misplaced.

5. Here is the three doughnuts that you wanted.

6. Five hundred dollars are the price that the dealer is asking.

7. Three-fourths of the pies have been eaten.

8. The majority of the state is Republican.

9. A golden retriever is one of those dogs that is always faithful.

10. Every one of the dancers is very limber.

11. The original document, as well as subsequent copies, was lost.

12. Neither the ashtray nor the lamp were on the table.

13. Only forty percent of the eligible voters is going to the polls.

14. Almost all of the newspaper are devoted to advertisements.

15. There are maps hanging on the walls.

16. Here is Shanna and Jessie.

17. The anguish of the victims have gone unnoticed.

18. Taxes on interest is still deferrable.

19. Neither he nor I are going.

20. Is it possible that Jose, as well as his family, are missing?

21. Five dollars are all I have to my name.

22. Neither of the lawyers are willing to take the case.

23. Each of the vacation homes are furnished with pots and pans.

Pronouns Quiz 1

Choose the correct pronoun(s) for each sentence. Answers are on page 120.

1. She/Her went to the store.

2. It was she/her.

3. We talked to he/him.

4. It is I/me.

5. Talk to they/them before making a decision.

6. Can you go with we/us?

7. Saleha and she/her have quit the team.

8. They asked he/him and I/me to join the staff.

9. That call was for I/me, not he/him.

10. You didn't tell we/us that they/them were here first.

11. I/me wonder what he/him could have said to she/her.

12. A message arrived for he/him and she/her.

13. Tell Imran and she/her that I/me called.

14. I am as willing as he/him to work hard.

15. She invited he/him to be her escort.

16. Erykah called Damjana and I/me as soon as she could.

17. It is they/them.

18. Beverly is more nervous than she/her.

19. It will be we/us who win this election.

20. Kathleen invited Lester and I/me to the movie.

21. This is he/him speaking.

Pronouns Quiz 2

Fix any pronoun errors in the following sentences. Place a check mark in front of sentences that are correct. Answers are on page 121.

1. Meagan said she looked forward to seeing he and I at the airport.

2. Him and me have been good friends since second grade.

3. If you don't mind me asking, why are you so angry?

4. My friend, unlike myself, is very artistic.

5. Please talk to Daniela or myself next time you have a concern.

6. Ask her, not me.

7. None of the doctors have been able to figure out what is wrong with she or I.

8. She is as stubborn as him, but that's no surprise given they are sister and brother.

9. I weigh more than him.

10. I would rather work with Raven than with her.

11. It is us who deserve credit for this company's third quarter profits.

12. Its a shame that some of the profits have been wasted on excessive executive compensation packages.

13. Him complaining just made everyone else more frustrated.

14. I and my friend will stop by on our way to the bakery.

15. You can help him or me but probably not both of us.

16. We regret to inform you that you running the red light has resulted in a ticket.

17. My boss and me will pick up where they left off.

18. When the horse kicked it's legs, the rider bounced off and landed in the lake.

19. You're friend told his' friend to tell my friend that their's a party tonight.

20. The argument he gave had it's merits.

Who, Whom, Whoever, Whomever Quiz 1

Choose the correct word for each sentence. Answers are on page 122.

1. _____ is your closest friend?

2. _____ do you bank with?

3. _____ do you think will win the award?

4. Clare knows _____ the winner is already.

5. Omar will talk about his girlfriend with _____ asks him.

6. Kimiko donates her time to _____ needs it most.

7. Quinton will work on the project with _____ you suggest.

8. _____ was that in the clown costume?

9. Kathy was not sure _____ she was voting for.

10. _____ wins the lottery will become a millionaire.

11. He is the man _____ was employed here.

12. She is the woman _____ we employed last year.

13. Of _____ were you speaking?

14. _____ do you think will do the work best?

15. He is the man _____ we think you mentioned.

16. I will vote for _____ you suggest.

17. _____ shall I ask about this matter?

18. Give the information to _____ requests it.

19. Tonight we shall find out _____ won.

20. _____ runs this show?

Who, Whom, Whoever, Whomever <u>Quiz 2</u>

Choose the correct word for each sentence. Answers are on page 123.

1. We intend to notify _____ ranks highest on the list.

2. These are the sign language interpreters _____ I feel you should acknowledge.

3. _____ can we trust in a crisis?

4. Ms. Cohen, _____ has a way with words, will be the valedictorian.

5. The person _____ produces the most work will receive a bonus.

6. _____ are you dancing with next?

7. _____ would you say is the best person for this position?

8. The therapist will talk with _____ needs her help.

9. We are not sure _____ set off the alarm.

10. Don't talk with anyone _____ you think might be connected with the competition.

11. _____ had my job before me?

12. It was she _____ they selected for the Cabinet post.

13. Sometimes it is the one _____ does the most work who is the least tired.

14. We plan to hire an assistant _____ is a good proofreader.

15. The prize will be given to _____ writes the best essay.

16. The bookkeeper is the one to _____ the figures should be mailed.

17. Give the recipe for the vegetarian chili to _____ calls for it.

18. _____ did you really want to be there?

19. She is the contestant _____ they sent to us.

20. This vacation spot will refresh _____ seeks refuge here.

Who, Whom, That, Which Quiz 1

Correct *who, whom, that,* or *which* in the following sentences. Place a check mark in front of sentences that are correct. Answers are on page 124.

1. Ahmed is the skydiver **that** broke his back last week.

2. That is a problem **that** can't be solved without a calculator.

3. That is a promise **which** cannot be broken.

4. The domino theory, **that** stated that, when one country fell to Communism, others in the area would likely fall, was used as an argument to continue the Vietnam War.

5. The game **which** intrigues Gretchen the most is dominoes.

6. Gandhi, **who** was a role model for nonviolence to millions, was assassinated.

7. The tomatoes **which** grow in her garden are unlike those you buy in a store.

8. The tomatoes from her garden, **which** grew larger than those in the grocery store, were sweet and ripe.

9. The baker **that** baked that bread should win an award.

Who, Whom, That, Which Quiz 2

Correct *who, whom, that,* or *which* in the following sentences. Place a check mark in front of sentences that are correct. Answers are on page 124.

1. Books have been written **which** address the horrors of the Salem witch trials.

2. That book, **that** was discovered in the basement of the library, will be published next year.

3. That is a book **which** I have not yet read.

4. The state law **which** banned logging ancient redwoods was put on the ballot by voter initiative.

5. The campaign to protect ancient redwoods, **which** began at the grass-roots level, has gained the attention of lawmakers at the national level.

6. The wheelchairs in that corner, **which** are motorized, are helpful to those who live in urban areas.

7. The people **that** are on my list haven't shown up yet.

8. The couple, **which** are my parents, left the party an hour ago.

9. Officer, he is the one **that** stole my purse.

Adjectives and Adverbs <u>Quiz 1</u>

Decide whether the words in bold are being used correctly. If not, change them. Place a check mark in front of sentences that are correct. Answers are on page 125.

1. Come **quick** or we will miss our bus.

2. You drive so **slow** that I am afraid someone will hit the car from behind.

3. I have never been **more surer** of anything in my life.

4. Ella was the **best** of the two sisters at gymnastics.

5. You did that somersault so **good**.

6. Rochelle felt **badly** about forgetting Devlin's birthday.

7. This is the **worst** oil spill I have ever seen.

8. The jasmine has bloomed and smells very **sweet**.

9. You look **angrily**. What did I do?

10. She looked **suspiciously** at the man wearing the trench coat.

11. **These** tree looks as though it is infested with beetles.

12. **Those** bushes need to be trimmed.

13. When was the last time you had no allergy symptoms and felt **good**?

14. In the library, you have to be **more quieter then** when you are outside.

15. She felt **good** about getting her puppy from the SPCA.

16. Charlotte has a **more better** approach to solving that problem.

17. Which is the **worst**, a toothache or a headache?

18. She reacted **swift**, which made him feel **badly** about insulting her.

19. The herbs in the salad tasted **bitter**.

20. Sharon fought **bitterly** against her ex-husband for custody of their daughter.

Adjectives and Adverbs Quiz 2

Decide whether the words in bold are being used correctly. If not, change them. Place a check mark in front of sentences that are correct. Answers are on page 125.

1. We are **real** happy to be of service to you and your family.

2. The perfume smells **sweetly**.

3. I feel **bad** about what happened.

4. Of all the holidays, this is the **most** joyful.

5. This wine tastes **dryly** to me.

6. Don't feel too **badly** about what you said.

7. This leotard hugs me **firmly**.

8. Life in the city is exciting, but life in the country is **best**.

9. If you don't speak **clear**, the audience will not understand you.

10. The **sweet** smell of roses has no match.

11. Walk **slow** or you will be sorry.

12. You don't look as though you feel **well** today.

13. You don't look as though you are doing **well** today.

14. My son doesn't feel very **good** today.

15. She was the **most** beautiful of the two.

16. The dentist said, "I will be finished drilling **real** soon."

17. Speak **slower** or you will lose your audience.

18. Juanita said she had better memories of Paris **then** of Rome.

19. If you won't tell me your secret now, **than** when will you tell me?

20. I would rather have hope **than** hold despair.

Problems with Prepositions <u>Quiz 1</u>

Correct the following sentences by adding, removing, or changing the prepositions. Place a check mark in front of sentences that are correct. Answers are on page 126.

1. Our ship leaves August 15.
2. I could of danced all night.
3. Where did you get this from?
4. If we split it evenly between the three of us, no one will be unhappy.
5. You can't just walk in the house without knocking.
6. He will be back the tenth.
7. Take your plate off of the table.
8. Cut the pie up into six slices.
9. Like the invitation stated, we'll see you the tenth for our reunion.
10. I don't know what you are talking about.
11. You could of told me about the mistake earlier.
12. I don't know where he is at or I would tell you.

Problems with Prepositions <u>Quiz 2</u>

Correct the following sentences by adding, removing, or changing the prepositions. Place a check mark in front of the sentences that are correct. Answers are on page 127.

1. Tell me where you found this at.
2. Sami will meet him May 18 at the Washington Hotel in downtown Seattle.
3. I should of known he would steal money from my purse.
4. We hiked into the woods and fell off of a log while crossing a creek.
5. That lie is still coming between the two of them.
6. Like I said, I am sorry for the muddy prints her paws left on the carpet.
7. I should of wiped her paws first.
8. The robbery happened just like you said it did.
9. She is the most enthusiastic student a teacher could hope for.
10. His brother's birthday is June 14.

11. Please take off your shoes when you come in.

12. Where did she go to?

Affect vs. Effect Quiz 1

Circle the correct word. Answers are on page 127.

1. The affect/effect of the antibiotic on her infection was surprising.

2. I did not know that antibiotics could affect/effect people so quickly.

3. Plastic surgery had an affect/effect, not only on her appearance, but on her self-esteem.

4. If the chemotherapy has no affect/effect, should she get surgery for the tumor?

5. When will we know if the chemotherapy has taken affect/effect?

6. Losing her hair from chemotherapy did not affect/effect her as much as her friends had expected.

7. We cannot affect/effect a new policy without the board of directors voting on it first.

8. To be an affective/effective leader, you should know both your strengths as well as your weaknesses.

9. The movie *Winged Migration* had two affects/effects on him: He became an environmental advocate and a bird lover.

10. The net affect/effect of blowing the whistle on her boss was that she was eventually given his position.

11. What was the affect/effect of his promotion?

12. His decision affected/effected everyone here.

13. We had to affect/effect a reduction in costs.

14. The critics greatly affected/effected his thinking.

15. How were you able to affect/effect such radical changes?

16. That book had a major affect/effect on his philosophy.

Affect vs. Effect Quiz 2

Circle the correct word. Answers are on page 128.

1. Shelley had to affect/effect great reductions in her expenses.

2. What do you suppose the affect/effect of her resignation will be?

3. The changes had an enormous affect/effect on production.

4. The crisis has greatly affected/effected our lifestyle.

5. They were able to affect/effect an increase in their savings.

6. Roberta has affected/effected many improvements in office procedures.

7. The rainy weather had a bad affect/effect on attendance at the seminar.

8. The new personnel ruling does not affect/effect my status.

9. The new director will reorganize the office and affect/effect a number of changes in personnel.

10. What she said had no affect/effect on the boss.

11. I don't know why the cold air affects/effects my skin.

12. I hope to affect/effect improvements in my work.

13. The knowledge I gain from this course will affect/effect my performance.

14. The new schedule will take affect/effect in October.

15. The supervisor affected/effected a reconciliation between Donya and Dayne.

16. The new law goes into affect/effect tomorrow.

Lay vs. Lie Quiz 1

Make corrections where needed. Place a check mark in front of sentences that are correct. Answers are on page 128.

1. I am dizzy and need to **lay** down.

2. When I got dizzy yesterday, I **laid** down.

3. My brother **lays** carpet for a living.

4. **Lay** the carpet after painting the walls.

5. We need to **lie** this baby down for a nap.

6. We will know when we have **lain** this issue to rest when we no longer fight about it.

7. The lions are **laying** in wait for their prey.

8. The lions have **laid** in wait for their prey.

9. I **laid** the blanket over her as she slept.

10. I will **lie** my head on my pillow shortly.

Lay vs. Lie <u>Quiz 2</u>

Make corrections where needed. Place a check mark in front of sentences that are correct. Answers are on page 129.

1. **Lay** down next to me and I will hold you.

2. When my dog is tired, she **lays** on her back.

3. I think we can **lay** the groundwork for lasting changes within the organization.

4. I have **laid** down because of a headache every afternoon this week.

5. Henry has **lied** consistently on the witness stand.

6. Sandra has **lain** out her plan for reorganization.

7. The preschoolers have **lain** down after lunch each day.

8. After I took the pill, I had to **lay** down.

9. I have **laid** my cards on the table.

10. **Lay** on this lounge chair and soak up some sun.

Advice vs. Advise <u>Quiz 1</u>

Circle the correct word. The answers are on page 129.

1. Adele is always happy to offer advice/advise if you ask her for it.

2. The lawyer adviced/advised him to plead guilty.

3. If you want to go on the senior trip, I would strongly advice/advise you to start saving your money.

4. Our new members are impressed with the level of advice/advise they received from the leadership group.

5. Sara always takes my advice/advise to heart.

6. I'd like to ask an engineer to advice/advise us on the design.

7. We adviced/advised the city council that the deadline was tentative and might need to be extended.

8. Lakeisha knows she can always go to her best friend for advice/advise.

9. Don't give advice/advise that you're not willing to follow yourself.

10. Randall has a bad habit of offering unsolicited advice/advise.

Advice vs. Advise <u>Quiz 2</u>

Circle the correct word. The answers are on page 130.

1. You can offer me advice/advise, but that doesn't mean I will follow it.
2. Paolo will give advice/advise to anyone, including complete strangers.
3. Next time I need financial advice/advise, I think I'll call Jerome.
4. From the beginning, she advice/advised me that the project would require fast turnaround times.
5. It's essential that we find a professional to advice/advise us on this situation.
6. I'm sure that Adriana will give careful consideration to your advice/advise.
7. It's important to interact with others in your industry to exchange ideas and advice/advise.
8. I strongly advice/advise you to call your doctor immediately.
9. The policeman adviced/advised him of his rights while placing the handcuffs around his wrists.
10. Mark won't mind if you call to ask his advice/advise about this.

Their vs. There vs. They're <u>Quiz 1</u>

Circle the correct word. The answers are on page 130.

1. According to an old legend, their/there/they're is treasure buried on that island.
2. Juan and Pancho just called to let us know their/there/they're coming for dinner.
3. Their/There/They're is a mouse in my closet!
4. I can't wait to see the looks on their/there/they're faces when I tell them the truth.
5. I wonder if their/there/they're planning to go shopping with us.
6. The children went upstairs to play after clearing their/there/they're plates at dinner.
7. It's their/there/they're decision, so I'll just stay out of it.
8. I don't know what their/there/they're doing to cause all that noise, but it's giving me a headache!

9. The kids haven't called yet; I'm concerned about their/there/they're being out so late at night.

10. I believe Wynona left her glasses over their/there/they're.

Their vs. There vs. They're <u>Quiz 2</u>

Circle the correct word. The answers are on page 131.

1. Do you see the bird's nest over their/there/they're?

2. I don't appreciate their/there/they're ignoring me when I speak to them.

3. I'm not sure where their/there/they're planning to hold the company picnic this year.

4. It's their/there/they're truck; I'm just borrowing it for the day.

5. The students were instructed to put down their/there/they're pencils after finishing the exam.

6. Their/There/They're baking the turkey for tonight's dinner.

7. You should have seen the shock in their/there/they're eyes when I won the award.

8. Their/There/There is a telephone down the hall.

9. Have Paige and Preston called to say whether their/there/they're going to the school play?

10. I was told that their/there/they're would be a free breakfast this morning.

More Confusing Words and Homonyms <u>Quiz 1</u>

Circle the correct word. The answers are on page 131.

1. Many people don't stop to consider how current events affect their every day/everyday lives.

2. I hope the solar flair/flare doesn't affect our computer equipment.

3. It's amazing that hangars/hangers can be built large enough to accommodate today's gigantic airplanes.

4. We'll need a forklift to place all those boxes on the palate/palette/pallet.

5. Would you like to have a sneak peak/peek/pique at the restaurant before it opens?

6. Use the rains/reigns/reins to guide the horse along the path.

7. The company will have to raise/raze adequate funds before it can move forward with the project.

8. My grandmother taught me how to sew/so/sow when I was a little girl.

9. Have you ever watched someone shear/sheer a sheep?

10. I'd like to go to the state fair on Sundae/Sunday.

11. If you ask her, Katerina will admit that she's quite vain/vane/vein.

12. We'll need to have a custom yoke/yolk built for the oxen.

13. Everyone is planning to go on the trip accept/except Dolores.

14. We are all ready/already for summer vacation.

15. Some religious leaders burn incense at an altar/alter as a form of prayer.

16. It will be easier to move the cabinet if you hold it at the base/bass.

17. If you ever come in contact with a wild boar/bore, do not provoke it.

18. Please be careful not to brake/break the vase.

19. Canvas/Canvass fabric is known for its durability, so I'd recommend using it for your project.

20. She ate the carat/carrot/karat raw.

More Confusing Words and Homonyms Quiz 2

Circle the correct word. Answers are on page 132.

1. He used the information from several of Heidi's newsletters, but he didn't cite/sight/site his sources.

2. She wasn't interested in being part of any of the clicks/cliques at school.

3. We have different specialties, so our business services complement/compliment one another.

4. I'm planning to have the chocolate cake for desert/dessert.

5. Many countries use questionable techniques to elicit/illicit information from their prisoners.

6. Carlos can't wait to go to the fair/fare this weekend.

7. We hired professionals to clean out our chimney flu/flue.

8. After screaming at the concert, Kamilah's voice was hoarse/horse.

9. The bolt of lightening/lightning struck the house and started a fire.

10. These pants are loose/lose, so I must have lost weight.

11. You know better than to medal/meddle/metal/mettle in other people's business.

12. I would like a chocolate moose/mousse cake for my birthday.

13. Armando left the other oar/or/ore in the canoe.

14. Casey looked pail/pale, so I thought she might be sick.

15. Having life insurance gives us peace/piece of mind.

16. Before hanging the wallpaper, check to see if the walls are plum/plumb.

17. We couldn't believe the squirrel climbed up that pole/poll.

18. When we opened the trash can, it reeked/wreaked of rotten meat.

19. Obtaining a driver's license is often considered a right/rite/write of passage.

20. When Marie's plane hadn't arrived, her mother started ringing/wringing her hands in worry.

More Confusing Words and Homonyms Quiz 3

Circle the correct word. The answers are on page 133.

1. The magician impressed the audience with his sleight/slight of hand.

2. Connie ordered her business stationary/stationery from the local print shop.

3. Dominic threw/through the garbage bag into the dumpster.

4. Even though Kurt asked my opinion, he didn't want to listen to my advice/advise.

5. Who's/Whose job is it to clean the kitchen tonight?

6. Until Simon called, I had almost given up on this deal all together/altogether.

7. A few days ago, Taya called to request my assistance/assistants with her latest project.

8. Many people are hesitant to bare/bear their souls on the Internet.

9. Students have a hard time remembering that the capital/capitol of California is Sacramento.

10. One day I'd like to go scuba diving and photograph the choral/chorale/coral/corral reefs.

11. When you sand any wood surface, always start with coarse/course sandpaper.

12. I wasn't at all surprised when Cindy decided to join the U.S. Marine Core/Corps.

13. Every time I try to sneak up on you, the floor creaks/creeks.

14. Please let Ricardo know when you're done with that project so you're not just sitting there idle/idol/idyl.

15. Irregardless/Regardless of Anita's recent illness, she still maintains a positive attitude.

16. Juanita lead/led the policemen to the place where she had parked her car.

17. If you'll give me a knife, I'll pair/pare/pear the apple.

18. Denise isn't known for her patience/patients with children.

19. There's an open market outside of town where merchants can pedal/peddle their goods.

20. This is the fifth time that Josef has been called to the principal's/principle's office.

Effective Writing Quiz 1

Rewrite these sentences to make them more effective. Your sentences may be different from the answers given in the book. Answers are on page 134.

1. We are no longer able to reconcile; therefore, attorneys will be used to effect the dissolution of our marriage.

2. The weather had adverse impacts on our boat resulting in the necessity to rescue us from the water.

3. The leak in the bottom of the boat was due to poor maintenance on the part of the crew.

4. Our marriage ended in a divorce.

5. The boy was struck in the face by the pie as it flew from the girl's hand.

6. It was not likely that no one would want to claim ownership of the new sports car.

7. There are many ideas that are worth exploring by us at this meeting.

8. Martin could not find time to work, shop, and go for walks with the dogs.

9. Jordan did not believe that Serena had embarrassed him unintentionally.

10. It is a shame that there are so many holidays that go uncelebrated.

11. While singing in the shower, the bar of soap slipped from her hands.

12. Looking back, the dog was following us.

13. Lying on a stretcher, they carried him out.

14. Flying out the window, he grabbed the papers.

15. Stepping off the bus, the shopping center was just ahead.

Effective Writing Quiz 2

Change the following sentences to make them more effective. Answers are on page 135.

1. It is necessary that you not be uninformed about this case.

2. There is ample evidence which indicates that the attorneys for the defense did not provide inadequate counseling to their client.

3. Speaking and to listen well are important elements of communication.

4. To win is the obvious goal, but playing fair is important too.

5. They were charged with assault, robbery, and forging checks.

6. I remember his generosity and that he was considerate.

7. She worked quickly and in an efficient manner.

8. When working with power tools, eyes should be protected.

9. When changing a diaper, a baby should be on his or her back.

10. I have some letters the mail carrier delivered in my purse.

11. We have tuna casserole I made in the refrigerator.

12. Mollie came over while I was playing the piano with a piece of pound cake.

13. While asleep, the flea bit the dog.

14. I tried calling to tell you about that TV show five times.

15. Although very spicy, Dana managed to finish the enchilada.

Grammar Mastery Test

Correct the following sentences. Answers are on page 136.

1. Some of the desserts was left by the end of the birthday party.

2. The papa bear thought that some of his porridge were missing.

3. Your brilliant excuses almost makes up for your tardiness.

4. Neither Jackson nor Jenna is playing hooky.

5. Neither Jackson nor I are playing hooky.

6. Either of us is capable of winning.

7. All of the class is willing to take part in the prank.

8. One-third of the eligible population tend not to vote in national elections.

9. One-third of the voters tends not to cast their ballots in national elections.

10. Here's the paper clips you requested.

11. She is one of those doctors who make house calls.

12. Dr. Cresta is one of those professors who does whatever it takes to get his point across to his students.

13. She is the only professor who does what it takes to help her students learn joyfully.

14. Her and him are always fighting.

15. When Toni and him come over, we always have a great time.

16. It is we who must decide whether to tax ourselves or cut spending.

17. Between you and I, this class is a joke.

18. Who do you think you are to give me advice about dating?

19. Who makes up these English rules anyway?

20. Whom do you think should win?

21. Who are you voting for?

22. Whoever has the keys gets to be in the driver's seat.

23. We are willing to work with whoever you recommend.

24. The thoughts that Ted presented at the meeting were so worthwhile.

25. The thoughts that Ted presented, that were about shifting national priorities, were well received.

26. When you do a job so good, you can expect a raise.

27. Bonnie was a good sport about losing the race.

28. Harry smells good. What is the aftershave he is wearing?

29. Lisa did so well on the test that she was allowed to accelerate to the next level.

30. Our puppy is definitely more sweeter than her brother.

31. With triplets, I have to be careful to divide everything equally between them or they will fight.

32. Karen should of known that her cheap umbrella would break in the storm.

33. Sometimes the effects of our generosity may seem minimal, but our good intentions do make a difference.

34. Ben thought he had lain my jacket on that bench.

35. Our company policy will not allow me to except a gift worth more than $50.

36. They thought we were late, but my wife and I were all ready at the restaurant.

37. Irregardless of who was there first, we were all very hungry and ready to eat.

38. We could hardly believe that the Giants could loose the game by that many runs.

39. Isn't it amazing how long that mime can remain completely stationary?

40. The department's principal concern is the safety of all employees.

41. How did they manage to serve cold ice cream in the middle of the vast dessert?

42. The boss complimented Ari on his excellent presentation.

43. The judge did not believe any of they're stories.

44. Ilana said she wanted to become a FBI agent when she grew up.

45. The meeting attendees were to express a preference between five cleanup plans.

46. To be a good billiards player, you've got to think farther ahead than just the next shot.

47. Paul should of known better than to act like that.

48. The golf course at the resort is lovely, but I prefer it's swimming pool.

49. I paid the cab fare and Alejandro paid for dinner.

50. Marta completed five less problems than I did in the same amount of time.

Punctuation, Capitalization, and Writing Numbers <u>Pretest</u>

Correct any errors in punctuation, capitalization, or writing numbers. Place a check mark in front of sentences that are correct. Answers are on page 138.

1. Go West three blocks and turn right.

2. Yes; sir, I will do it immediately.

3. "How," I asked "Can you always be so forgetful"?

4. The woman, who is standing there, is his ex-wife.

5. Although we have a competent staff; bottlenecks do occur.

6. I did not receive the order; therefore, I will not pay my bill.

7. We offer a variety of drinks, for instance, beer.

8. Is that book your's?

9. We have much to do, for example, the carpets need vacuuming.

10. Estimates for the work have been forwarded, and a breakdown of costs has been included.

11. Because of his embezzling the company went bankrupt.

12. A proposal that makes harassment of whales illegal has just passed.

13. You may; of course, call us anytime you wish.

14. Paolo hurried to the depot to meet his aunt, and two cousins.

15. Finish your job, it is imperative that you do.

16. Sofia and Aidan's house was recently painted.

17. "Stop it!" I said, "Don't ever do that again."

18. I would; therefore like to have an explanation for the missing cash.

19. ''Would you like to accompany me''? he asked?

20. I have always had a mental block against Math.

21. He is a strong healthy man.

22. To apply for this job you must have previous experience.

23. Marge, the woman with blonde hair will be our speaker this evening.

24. He thought quickly, and then answered the question in complete detail.

25. He asked if he could be excused?

26. It is hailing; not raining.

27. We will grant you immunity, if you decide to cooperate with us.

28. You signed the contract, consequently you must provide us with the raw materials.

29. I would like; however, to read the fine print first.

30. You are required to bring the following: Sleeping bag, food, and a sewing kit.

31. The three companie's computers were stolen.

32. The womens' department is upstairs and to your left.

33. It hurt it's paw.

34. One of the lawyer's left her briefcase.

35. ''What does it take to become a licensed architect,'' she asked?

36. I can't remember if her birthday falls on a Saturday, Sunday or Monday next year.

37. I need to locate four states on the map; Arkansas, Ohio, Illinois, and Utah.

38. The email read, ''Hi Camille. I haven't heard from you in two weeks.''

39. The veterinarian said, ''Unless its bleeding and doesn't stop, don't worry about it.''

40. In letting go of needing to discuss this with her mother anymore, Wendy declared, ''This is her karma not mine.''

41. You must study hard, to get good grades at a major university.

42. 1/4 of the police force voted for a pay raise.

43. Whether Bella has five students or fifteen students, she will give the test.

44. I owe you $15.00, not $16.

Commas <u>Quiz 1</u>

Correct any comma errors. Place a check mark in front of sentences that are correct. Answers are on page 140.

1. I took Angie the one with the freckles to the movie last night.
2. Jeremy, and I, have had our share of arguments.
3. You are I am sure, telling the truth.
4. She left Albany, New York on January 18 of that year.
5. I need sugar, butter, and eggs, from the grocery store.
6. Please Sasha, come home as soon as you can.
7. Although you may be right I cannot take your word for it.
8. We will grant you immunity if you decide to cooperate with us.
9. I am typing a letter and she is talking on the phone.
10. She finished her work, and then took a long lunch.
11. Mae said "Why don't you come up and see me sometime?"
12. You said that I could go, didn't you?
13. To apply for this job you must have a Social Security card.
14. He seems to be such a lonely, quiet man doesn't he?
15. She wore a brightly colored dress.
16. She has a good healthy attitude about her work.

Commas <u>Quiz 2</u>

Correct any comma errors. Place a check mark in front of sentences that are correct. Answers are on page 140.

1. Girls, who have red hair, are very lucky.
2. He asked where his hat was.
3. They are, one might say, true believers.
4. Cheryl arrived in Denver Colorado, hoping to find a good job.
5. On July 20, 1969 astronauts landed on the moon for the first time.
6. Life, liberty and the pursuit of happiness are three guarantees granted to us by our forefathers.
7. I told you Jesse, never to ask me that question again.
8. I may as well not speak if you refuse to even listen.

9. I am already finished cooking but he has not taken his shower yet.

10. I walked all the way to the bus stop and waited for a bus for over an hour.

11. It is drizzling not pouring.

12. What a delicious, appetizing meal!

13. Dario drove to the airport to meet his wife and children.

14. Yes I can be ready in five minutes.

15. I will not stop you, if you want to leave.

16. Rosie Hernandez Ph.D. will be our guest speaker.

Semicolons and Colons **Quiz 1**

Correct any comma, semicolon, or colon errors. Some sentences may require removing punctuation. Place a check mark in front of sentences that are correct. Answers are on page 141.

> ***Example:***   *We told Annika that we would take three courses next fall;*
> *French, American Literature, and Advanced Algebra.*
>
> ***Correction:*** *We told Annika that we would take three courses next fall:*
> *French, American Literature, and Advanced Algebra.*

1. You asked for forgiveness, he granted it to you.

2. We ask; therefore, that you keep this matter confidential.

3. The order was requested six weeks ago, therefore I expected the shipment to arrive by now.

4. The American flag has three colors, namely, red, white, and blue.

5. Clothes are often made from synthetic material; for instance, rayon.

6. If you believe in magic, magical things will happen, but if you do not believe in magic, you will discover nothing to be magical.

7. The orchestra, excluding the violin section; was not up to par.

8. I have been to San Francisco, California, Reno, Nevada, and Seattle, Washington.

9. I need a few items at the store; clothespins, a bottle opener, and napkins.

10. I answered the phone; but no one seemed to be on the other end of the line.

11. I wanted a cup of coffee, not a glass of milk.

12. You have won the following prizes: namely, a car, a trip to Hawaii, and a bathrobe.

13. If you can possibly arrange it, please visit us, but if you cannot, let us know.

14. I gave her a lot of money while we were married hence I do not wish to pay her a dime in alimony.

15. We have a variety of desserts, for instance apple pie.

16. I needed only three cards to win, namely the ten of hearts, the jack of diamonds, and the king of hearts.

17. I needed only three cards to win; the ten of hearts, the jack of diamonds, and the king of hearts.

18. I would; therefore, like to have an explanation for the missing cash.

19. Nature lovers will appreciate seeing: whales, sea lions, and pelicans.

20. He has friends from Iowa and Nebraska and Illinois is his home state.

21. We have set this restriction, do your homework before watching television.

Semicolons and Colons Quiz 2

Correct any comma, semicolon, or colon errors. Some sentences may require removing punctuation. Place a check mark in front of sentences that are correct. Answers are on page 142.

> *Example:* *The recipe calls for: flour, butter, and sugar.*
> *Correction: The recipe calls for flour, butter, and sugar.*

1. He has friends from Montana Iowa and Nebraska and Illinois is his home state.

2. This is a difficult exercise but I am having fun.

3. Although this is a difficult exercise I am having fun.

4. This is a difficult exercise I am having fun though.

5. The man who is wearing dark glasses is an FBI undercover agent.

6. That FBI agent who is wearing dark glasses once protected the president.

7. Did you John eat my cake?

8. Did John eat my cake?

9. Did his friend John eat my cake?

10. Did John his friend eat the cake?

11. If everything goes according to plan he will retire at 40 if real estate prices continue to drop however he may have to work until he is 65.

12. Golden retrievers, which are known to be gentle are also loyal.

13. Dogs that are gentle are often good family pets.

14. I would love to be rich and famous although fame has mixed blessings.

15. I would love to be rich and famous and famous is the first priority.

16. She chose the field of journalism because of Nellie Bly the first woman reporter.

17. They built an adobe house but then they decided to move.

18. They built an adobe house but then decided to move.

19. They built an adobe house however they decided to move.

20. They built an adobe house because they decided never to move again.

21. Since they moved to the desert they decided to build an adobe house.

22. Mr. Liu held this belief, if he worked hard, he would be able to save enough money to travel to Madagascar and photograph rarely seen animals.

Question Marks, Quotation Marks, and Parentheses Quiz 1

Correct the punctuation errors in the following sentences. Answers are on page 143.

> **Example:** *He asked, ''Did Danika really say that''?*
> **Correction:** *He asked, ''Did Danika really say that?''*

1. He wanted to know when you will be here?

2. ''Well, she said, ''you certainly didn't waste any time.''

3. ''Is it almost over?'' he asked?

4. ''I've had it up to here!'', she screamed.

5. The song asks, ''Would you like to swing on a star''?

6. Carmen said, ''She said, ''I'll never leave you.''

7. She requested (actually she pleaded, that her name be withheld.

8. This contract guarantees that we will 1 deliver the merchandise, 2 pay for all damaged goods, and 3 make you the exclusive carrier of our products.

9. "May I have a rain check on that lunch"? I asked.

10. Do you believe the saying, "It is better to vote for what you want and not get it than to vote for what you don't want and get it?"

11. Bernard said, Waldo asked, "Who took my pencil sharpener?"

12. "May I see your I.D. card," the clerk asked?

Question Marks, Quotation Marks, and Parentheses Quiz 2

Correct the punctuation errors in the following sentences.

> **Example:**   *Fernando asked? "Where is my umbrella"?*
> **Correction:** *Fernando asked, "Where is my umbrella?"*

Answers are on page 144.

1. "Correct me if I am wrong." She said.

2. "Correct me if I am wrong" she said, "but don't you usually drive a truck?"

3. Sandi asked, "Did Jeri say, 'I am pregnant?'"

4. I can have lunch with you tomorrow (Friday.)

5. I hope you are feeling better (I am sick today.)

6. Did he ask? "Where are my keys"?

7. Harry needs to know if he can count on you?

8. I smiled (actually I laughed) when I saw the expression on his face.

9. Nicole said with shock in her voice! "I can't believe what I just saw."

10. It wouldn't surprise me if he quit his job?

11. I can't think of what to say?

12. Tessa thinks he said that "he would go to the movie with her."

Apostrophes Quiz 1

Correct any apostrophe errors. Answers are on page 144.

1. Her husbands wallet was full of curious, little items.

2. I went to my mother-in-law house for dinner last night.

3. You may not enter Mr. Harris office without his permission.

4. The girls vitality and humor were infectious. [one girl]

5. The womens dresses are on the second floor.

6. Its a shame that had to happen.

7. Its hard to believe that winter is almost here.

8. Her mother and father business went bankrupt.

9. It is his' word against mine.

10. The actresses costumes looked beautiful on them.

11. Sharon arriving was unexpected.

12. The movie had it's desired effect.

Apostrophes Quiz 2

Correct any apostrophe or errors with possession. Answers are on page 145.

1. His 6's and 8's looked alike.

2. Where would I find the mens room?

3. Both secretary vacations caused a delay in output.

4. New clients accounts showed an 11 percent increase in sales. (clients is plural)

5. Most children imaginations run wild when told that story.

6. Both son-in-law opinions were considered.

7. Several M.D. agreed that one bacterial strain caused many of the symptoms.

8. These M.D. credentials are excellent.

9. Both brother-in-law jobs required physical labor.

10. Do you mind me looking at the earrings in this jewelry case?

11. You're right to privacy will not be abused.

12. It's beauty is unsurpassed.

Hyphens Between Words Quiz 1

Add or remove hyphens as necessary. Place commas between adjectives that require them. Place a check mark in front of sentences that are correct. Answers are on page 145.

1. She jumped from a two story building.

2. The show's cancellation was a real letdown.

3. You must let-down your guard.

4. You certainly have a go get it nature.

5. What a cute little bird she has!

6. We offer around the clock coverage.

7. Look left-and-right before you cross the street.

8. The left handed pitcher threw fastballs at almost 100 miles per hour.

9. The delicious gooey frosting melted before we could refrigerate the cake.

10. Do you remember anything you read in the fourth grade?

11. This is seventh grade reading material.

12. Beware of high-pressure telemarketers.

Hyphens Between Words Quiz 2

Add or remove hyphens as necessary. Place commas between adjectives that require them. Place a check mark in front of sentences that are correct. Answers are on page 146.

1. Turn left after the big red door.

2. This is a one family dwelling.

3. Do you think he has above average intelligence?

4. I would like that antique picture frame.

5. She owns income producing property.

6. That is a well written letter.

7. If you are not satisfied, we will give you your money-back.

8. This product comes with a money back guarantee.

9. The highway patrol will crack-down on drunk drivers over the Memorial Day holiday.

10. Please let-up on your criticisms about my writing.

11. Paying a $100 fine for a speeding ticket was a wake up call.

12. The small-plastic lid seems to be missing.

Hyphens with -ly Words Quiz 1

Add or remove hyphens as necessary. Place a check mark in front of sentences that are correct. Answers are on page 146.

1. This appears to be a firmly built house.

2. A dimly lit restaurant can be rather romantic.

3. A friendly little dog is all I need for company.

4. The data was readily available.

5. He is a happily married man.

6. What kindly looking eyes my grandfather had.

7. If someone causes bodily-harm while defending herself, should she be prosecuted?

8. The tree was firmly-planted in the ground.

9. Noah's art work is positively beautiful.

10. Your award is richly-deserved.

Hyphens with -ly Words Quiz 2

Add or remove hyphens as necessary. Place commas between adjectives that require them. Place a check mark in front of sentences that are correct. Answers are on page 147.

1. You are certainly a likely looking prospect for the job.

2. A silly acting child is a joy to behold.

3. A chilly snowy morning would be a refreshing sight.

4. The lovely sounding music came from that singer over there.

5. The friendly acting dog growled whenever he had a bone nearby.

6. She appears to be happily married.

7. The smelly dirty dog shook the water off itself.

8. The scantily clad doll was pulled from the toy store's inventory.

9. Ella showed her carefully-prepared report to her supervisor.

10. Boris's goals are poorly defined.

Hyphens with Prefixes Quiz 1

Insert hyphens or close up the space where appropriate. Answers are on page 147.

1. anti aircraft

2. ultra anxious

3. anti depressant

4. anti freeze

5. anti impressionism

6. un patriotic

7. non professional

8. non existent

9. self paced

10. co operation

Hyphens with Prefixes <u>Quiz 2</u>

Insert hyphens or close up the space where appropriate. Answers are on page 147.

1. non Jewish

2. pre existing

3. re establish

4. self satisfied

5. ex Marine

6. anti inflammatory

7. anti war

8. un natural

9. non essential

10. bi ennial

Hyphens with <u>re-</u> Words <u>Quiz 1</u>

Insert hyphens or close up the space where appropriate. Answers are on page 148.

1. When can we re furnish our home?

2. Our friendship was re newed.

3. I cannot re collect the story.

4. Please re collect the papers, Mikaela.

5. That point should be re emphasized.

6. I enjoy re covering chairs.

7. Because of new DNA evidence, the police need to re solve the case.

8. I re sent your questioning my integrity.

9. Please re sign the documents you signed yesterday.

10. It takes a lot of re solve to eat nutritiously.

Hyphens with re- Words Quiz 2

Insert hyphens or close up space where appropriate. Answers are on page 148.

1. The astronauts began the re entry phase.

2. Martin Luther began the Re formation.

3. I made a mistake and had to re form the clay.

4. I must re press the wrinkled suit.

5. I will release the apartment after the current tenants leave. (lease again)

6. The couple was re united after a long separation.

7. It is not unusual to re press traumatic memories.

8. If he doesn't re press his slacks after unpacking, they will be rumpled.

9. Would you vote to re elect Senator Hogan?

10. His re served nature is often mistaken for aloofness.

Capitalization Quiz 1

Correct the following sentences if an error appears. Answers are on page 149.

1. She said, "bees are not the only insects that sting."

2. "You must understand," he pleaded, "That I need more time to pay you."

3. Mark Paxton, the Vice President of the company, embezzled over one million dollars.

4. The President of the United States wields much power.

5. I live in the northeastern part of the state where the climate is colder.

6. The West, especially California, is famous for its cutting-edge technology.

7. Have you read *All the King's Men*?

8. I enjoy Summer more than any other season.

9. Employees of the Company were laid off with little hope of returning to work.

10. My Dear Mr. Simpson:

11. Sincerely Yours,

Capitalization Quiz 2

Correct the following sentences if an error appears. Answers are on page 149.

1. I lived on Elm street a few years ago.

2. The American river is extremely cold all year.

3. Do not swim in that River because of the swift current.

4. "You must realize," he explained, "that my circumstances are desperate."

5. "Stop it!" she screamed. "don't ever do that again."

6. She said, "we strive hard for a better world, but we don't lift a finger for perfection."

7. The west has a milder climate than the east.

8. You must take the following courses: history, geometry, and french.

9. The supervisor will decide whether state regulations prohibit our taking Monday as a holiday.

10. My major requires that I take Calculus 1, History, and French.

11. The federal reserve board will raise interest rates over many State agencies' objections.

Writing Numbers Quiz 1

Make corrections to the numbers in the following sentences. Place a check mark in front of sentences that are correct. Answers are on page 150.

1. I asked for 2 copies each for my twelve employees.

2. If only 14 people show up, will you still make a speech?

3. One fifth of the inventory was ruined in the fire.

4. A 2/3 majority is needed to pass the measure.

5. The tree grew only .5 of an inch because of the drought.

6. He hit more home runs in '06 than in '05.

7. Her earnings rose from $500 to $5,000.00 in one year because of her marketing efforts.

8. We didn't get to bed until 11:30 last night.

9. At exactly 11:33, the phone rang.

10. 47 people were hired last month.

Writing Numbers Quiz 2

Make corrections to the numbers in the following sentences. The answers are on page 150.

1. If you let her nap for 2 hours, she will be up until midnight.

2. His company grew from seven employees to thirty-seven employees in 4 months.

3. A .9% profit is not the same as a 9% profit.

4. The hotel woke us up at 6 o'clock.

5. A 7:40 o'clock bedtime for a toddler sounds about right.

6. Please send me a reimbursement for two hundred and thirty three dollars.

7. 10% of insomniacs are also sleepwalkers.

8. For just 5 dollars more per month, you can have your checks deposited directly into your account.

9. A .05 cent postage increase is set for May.

10. 1/3 of an adult's body is made up of water.

Punctuation, Capitalization, and Writing Numbers <u>Mastery Test</u>

Correct any errors in punctuation, capitalization, or writing numbers. Place a check mark in front of sentences that are correct. Answers are on page 151.

1. I am asking if you would like to rollerblade together tomorrow?

2. Yes Jean, you were right about that answer.

3. I read in a book, "If all else fails, succeed; if all else succeeds . . ."

4. Wherever we go people recognize us.

5. Whenever Cheryl is in town she visits her sister.

6. Isabel enjoys the museum although she cannot afford the entrance fee.

7. It may not be the correct part but I bet that it works.

8. You are my friend, however, I cannot afford to lend you any more money.

9. Paul Simon sang, "I am a rock, I am an island."

10. I asked Ella, "Did he ask for his ring back"?

11. John F. Kennedy, Jr. became a magazine publisher and a pilot before his tragic death.

12. Please contact me if you have any questions.

13. The elections will be held on the first Tuesday of November 2008.

14. The elections, will be held on Tuesday, November 4, 2008, and the polls will be kept open until 8:00 P.M.

15. Carl worried about the hurricane but tried to stay calm and help his family.

16. I favor green and yellow and purple is her first choice.

17. I need to locate four states on the map: namely, Minnesota, Michigan, California, and Nevada.

18. This is the point that Einstein made; You cannot fix a problem with the problem.

19. Our philosophy teacher thinks that Einstein meant that we cannot stop war by waging war.

20. A well made argument was presented for negotiating a peaceful resolution.

21. The argument for negotiating a peaceful resolution was well made.

22. A liberally sprinkled dose of humor was very much appreciated.

23. Our liberal minded clergyman managed to unite the entire congregation.

24. Our clergyman, who united the entire congregation, was liberal-minded.

25. Jan asked, "What did Joe mean when he said, 'I will see you later?'"

26. When I noticed that our dog cut it's paw, I called the veterinarian right away.

27. Just to be sure, I called three more D.V.M.'s offices.

28. "Your right to be concerned," said one veterinarian. "I would like to take a look at your dog."

29. Even though its 30 miles to the town where that D.V.M.'s office is, I wanted to take the drive.

30. The friendly looking vet examined our dog's paw and suggested that we have it bandaged.

31. We had pet insurance but still owed $40 in copayment fees.

32. Our dog was a semi-invalid for a couple of days until she chewed off the bandage.

33. I guess she did what any self respecting dog would do by grooming herself.

34. The dog has fully re-covered although I will never be the same.

35. I have learned that it's better to be pro-active than to have regrets.

36. Wendy thought she knew everything about her mother but found out two years ago that her mother had been married before.

37. When Wendy asked her mother about this marriage, Ilse (her mother) was hesitant to discuss any details.

38. She will go to her grave with some secrets said Wendy.

39. "Do you understand her need for privacy," Wendy asked her husband?

40. The wealthy became wealthier during the 1990s.

41. The alarm clock went off at 4:00 o'clock.

42. Many people dread the 15 of April.

43. The check was written for $13348.15.

44. The check was written for thirteen thousand three hundred forty eight dollars and fifteen cents.

Chapter 7

Answers to Quizzes

Grammar Pretest Answers

1. How quickly he runs.
2. Neither DeAndre nor I am to follow.
3. The desk and the chair sit in the corner.
4. Each of us was scheduled to take the test.
5. The coach, not the players, has been ill.
6. There are only four days until Christmas.
7. She is one of the women who work hard.
8. That was Yusuf and I whom you saw.
9. This phone call is for Bill and me.
10. Terrell is the smarter of the two.
11. It was I who called.
12. It is we clerks who work hard.
13. He took the plate off the table.
14. None of the neighbors offered their support.
15. They mailed the copies to him and me.
16. Neither of the candidates has spoken.
17. How will you be affected financially if the effect of downsizing means you will lose your job?

18. Joan walks slowly so her children can keep up with her. (**OR** *more slowly*)

19. Jake is the older of the two brothers.

20. May did well on the test she took yesterday.

21. He and she were really close friends. (**OR** *very*)

22. Whoever drove in the carpool lane without any passengers will be fined.

23. Please allow Jenna or me to assist you.

24. I work with people who judge others by their nationalities and accents.

25. They fought over their father's estate because they felt angry about the way he had treated them.

26. You look good in that running outfit.

27. Don't feel bad about forgetting my birthday.

28. We saw two puppies at the pound and took home the cuter one.

29. Speak more slowly please.

30. Samantha will meet us later.

31. Pollen affects my sinuses and makes me sneeze.

32. I want to lie down for a nap, but the phone keeps ringing.

33. That SUV, which landed on its hood after the accident, was traveling at eighty miles per hour.

34. Yesterday, Barry laid my jacket on the hood of the car.

35. How much farther before we arrive in Santa Fe?

36. My daughter became an honorary member of the city council for the day.

37. In the end, we had to decide between a minivan and a station wagon as our second car.

38. You're the only one for me.

39. That redwood tree has become taller than the oak tree next door.

40. The time for action has long since passed.

41. It's a long way from here to Tierra del Fuego.

42. Mother, may I go to the movies with Ashton this afternoon?

43. I could have danced all night.

44. Srdjian emigrated from his native Bosnia about five years ago.

45. I am tiring of the noise from the continuous flow of traffic past my apartment.

46. The teacher tried to elicit a discussion about the novel.

47. La Donna talks fondly about the four years that she went to the university.

48. The answer is plain and simple.

49. Let me set this book down on the table before I answer your question.

50. The legislature finally authorized the funds to polish the gold on the dome of the capitol building.

Finding Subjects and Verbs Quiz 1 Answers

1. He <u>depends</u> on her in times of need.

2. (You) <u>Watch</u> your step.

3. The insurance <u>agent gave</u> her sound advice.

4. On the table <u>was</u> her <u>purse</u>.

5. In the newspaper, an interesting <u>article appeared</u>.

6. (You) <u>Look</u> before <u>you leap</u>.

7. Across the road <u>lived</u> her <u>boyfriend</u>.

8. <u>We are forced</u> to inhale and exhale this smog-filled air. (or <u>are</u>)

9. In the gutter, <u>I found</u> a shiny new dime.

10. Around every cloud <u>is</u> a silver <u>lining</u>.

11. Every <u>one</u> of the roses <u>bloomed</u>.

Finding Subjects and Verbs Quiz 2 Answers

1. This gorgeous grand <u>piano is tuned</u> to perfection. (or <u>is</u>)

2. Every environmental <u>regulation has been undermined</u> by that industry. (or <u>has been</u>)

3. My <u>gift</u> for walking and talking simultaneously <u>did</u> not <u>go</u> unnoticed.

4. Your red <u>scarf matches</u> your eyes.

5. Every <u>attempt</u> to flatter him <u>failed</u> miserably.

6. (You) <u>Think</u> before <u>you speak</u> and <u>you will be</u> glad for the things <u>you</u> never <u>said</u>.

7. If <u>all is</u> lost, why <u>am</u> I still <u>playing</u>?

8. Jared <u>needed</u> a pity party after he <u>lost</u> his job.

9. <u>Have</u> <u>you</u> <u>memorized</u> all the chemical symbols on the chart?

10. *Buses* <u>has</u> only one *s* in the middle of it.

11. <u>(You)</u> Please <u>answer</u> the question without smirking.

Subject and Verb Agreement **Quiz 1 Answers**

1. At the end of the story, <u>they</u> <u>were living</u> happily ever after. (or <u>were</u>)

2. <u>Al</u> and <u>Eli</u> <u>go</u> to the beach to surf with their friends. (CORRECT)

3. When <u>Al</u> and <u>Eli</u> <u>arrive</u>, <u>they</u> <u>find</u> that their friends <u>have waxed</u> their boards.

4. The <u>group</u> of children from that school <u>has</u> never <u>seen</u> the ocean. (CORRECT or <u>don't quit picking</u>)

5. If our <u>staff</u> members <u>don't quit</u> picking at each other, <u>we</u> <u>will</u> not <u>meet</u> our goals. (CORRECT)

6. Either <u>Gary</u> or <u>I</u> <u>am</u> responsible for allocating the funds.

7. Neither <u>she</u> nor <u>they</u> <u>were willing</u> to predict the election results. (CORRECT or <u>were</u>)

8. <u>Nora</u> <u>is</u> one of the candidates <u>who</u> <u>are</u> worthy of my vote.

9. <u>Nora</u>, of all the candidates <u>who</u> <u>are running</u>, <u>is</u> the best. (or <u>are</u>)

10. My <u>problem</u>, <u>which</u> <u>is</u> minor in comparison with others, <u>exists</u> because <u>I</u> <u>dropped out</u> of high school.

11. His <u>dogs</u>, <u>which</u> <u>are kept</u> outside, <u>bark</u> all day long. (CORRECT)

12. There <u>are</u> three <u>strawberries</u> left.

13. Here <u>are</u> the <u>reports</u> from yesterday.

14. <u>Some</u> of my goals <u>have</u> yet to be met.

15. <u>All</u> of my goals <u>are being met</u> and <u>surpassed</u>. (CORRECT)

16. <u>None</u> of this <u>is</u> your business. (CORRECT)

17. <u>None</u> of them <u>are coming</u> home tonight.

18. <u>One-third</u> of the city <u>is experiencing</u> a blackout tonight.

19. <u>One-third</u> of the people <u>are suffering</u>. (CORRECT or <u>are</u>)

20. When <u>she</u> <u>talks</u>, <u>we</u> <u>listen</u>.

21. Neither the <u>farmer</u> nor the <u>farm workers</u> <u>are willing</u> to settle the strike. (or <u>are</u>)

22. Neither <u>Darren</u> nor <u>Ida</u> <u>is</u> <u>capable</u> of such a crime. (or <u>is</u>)

Subject and Verb Agreement Quiz 2 Answers

1. The <u>teacher</u> or <u>student</u> <u>is going</u> to appear on stage first. (CORRECT)
2. The mother <u>duck</u>, along with all her ducklings, <u>swims</u> so gracefully.
3. <u>Each</u> of those dresses <u>is</u> beautiful. (CORRECT)
4. The <u>folder</u>, not the letters, <u>was misplaced</u>. (or <u>was</u>)
5. Here <u>are</u> the three <u>doughnuts</u> that <u>you</u> <u>wanted</u>.
6. <u>Five hundred dollars</u> <u>is</u> the price that the <u>dealer</u> <u>is asking</u>.
7. <u>Three-fourths</u> of the pies <u>have been eaten</u>. (CORRECT)
8. The <u>majority</u> of the state <u>is</u> Republican. (CORRECT)
9. A <u>golden retriever</u> <u>is</u> one of those dogs <u>that</u> <u>are</u> always faithful.
10. Every <u>one</u> of the dancers <u>is</u> very limber. (CORRECT)
11. The original <u>document</u>, as well as subsequent copies, <u>was</u> lost. (CORRECT)
12. Neither the <u>ashtray</u> nor the <u>lamp</u> <u>was</u> on the table.
13. Only <u>forty percent</u> of the eligible voters <u>are</u> going to the polls. (or <u>are going</u>)
14. Almost <u>all</u> of the newspaper <u>is</u> devoted to advertisements.
15. There <u>are</u> maps <u>hanging</u> on the walls. (CORRECT or <u>are</u>)
16. Here <u>are</u> Shanna and Jessie.
17. The <u>anguish</u> of the victims <u>has gone</u> unnoticed. (or <u>has</u>)
18. <u>Taxes</u> on interest <u>are</u> still deferrable.
19. Neither <u>he</u> nor <u>I</u> <u>am going</u>.
20. <u>Is</u> it possible that <u>Jose</u>, as well as his family, <u>is</u> missing? (or <u>is missing</u>)
21. <u>Five dollars</u> <u>is</u> all I <u>have</u> to my name.
22. <u>Neither</u> of the lawyers <u>is</u> willing to take the case. (or <u>is willing</u>)
23. <u>Each</u> of the vacation homes <u>is</u> furnished with pots and pans.

Pronouns Quiz 1 Answers

1. **She** went to the store.
2. It was **she**. (This is preferred although using *her* is considered acceptable by some English teachers.)

3. We talked to **him**.

4. It is **I**. (Preferred over *me*.)

5. Talk to **them** before making a decision.

6. Can you go with **us**?

7. Saleha and **she** have quit the team.

8. They asked **him** and **me** to join the staff.

9. That call was for **me**, not **him**.

10. You didn't tell **us** that **they** were here first.

11. **I** wonder what **he** could have said to **her**.

12. A message arrived for **him** and **her**.

13. Tell Imran and **her** that **I** called.

14. I am as willing as **he** to work hard.

15. She invited **him** to be her escort.

16. Erykah called Damjana and **me** as soon as she could.

17. It is **they**. (Preferred over *them*.)

18. Beverly is more nervous than **she**.

19. It will be **we** who win this election. (Preferred over *us*.)

20. Kathleen invited Lester and **me** to the movie.

21. This is **he** speaking. (Preferred over *him*.)

Pronouns Quiz 2 Answers

1. Meagan said she looked forward to seeing **him** and **me** at the airport.

2. **He** and **I** have been good friends since second grade.

3. If you don't mind **my** asking, why are you so angry?

4. My friend, unlike **me**, is very artistic.

5. Please talk to Daniela or **me** next time you have a concern.

6. Ask her, not me. (CORRECT)

7. None of the doctors have been able to figure out what is wrong with **her** or **me**.

8. She is as stubborn as **he**, but that's no surprise given they are sister and brother.

9. I weigh more than **he**.

10. I would rather work with Raven than with her. (CORRECT)

11. It is **we** who deserve credit for this company's third quarter profits. (Preferred over *us*.)

12. **It's** a shame that some of the profits have been wasted on excessive executive compensation packages.

13. **His** complaining just made everyone else more frustrated.

14. **My friend** and **I** will stop by on our way to the bakery.

15. You can help him or me but probably not both of us. (CORRECT)

16. We regret to inform you that **your** running the red light has resulted in a ticket.

17. My boss and **I** will pick up where they left off.

18. When the horse kicked **its** legs, the rider bounced off and landed in the lake.

19. **Your** friend told **his** friend to tell my friend that **there's** (**OR** *there is*) a party tonight.

20. The argument he gave had **its** merits.

Who, Whom, Whoever, Whomever Quiz 1 Answers

1. **Who** is your closest friend?

2. **Whom** do you bank with? **OR** With **whom** do you bank?

3. **Who** do you think will win the award?

4. Clare knows **who** the winner is already.

5. Omar will talk about his girlfriend with **whoever** asks him.

6. Kimiko donates her time to **whoever** needs it most.

7. Quinton will work on the project with **whomever** you suggest.

8. **Who** was that in the clown costume?

9. Kathy was not sure **whom** she was voting for.

10. **Whoever** wins the lottery will become a millionaire.

11. He is the man **who** was employed here.

12. She is the woman **whom** we employed last year.

13. Of **whom** were you speaking?

14. **Who** do you think will do the work best?

15. He is the man **whom** we think you mentioned.

16. I will vote for **whomever** you suggest.

17. **Whom** shall I ask about this matter?

18. Give the information to **whoever** requests it.

19. Tonight we shall find out **who** won.

20. **Who** runs this show?

Who, Whom, Whoever, Whomever Quiz 2 Answers

1. We intend to notify **whoever** ranks highest on the list.

2. These are the sign language interpreters **whom** I feel you should acknowledge.

3. **Whom** can we trust in a crisis?

4. Ms. Cohen, **who** has a way with words, will be the valedictorian.

5. The person **who** produces the most work will receive a bonus.

6. **Whom** are you dancing with next?

7. **Who** would you say is the best person for this position?

8. The therapist will talk with **whoever** needs her help.

9. We are not sure **who** set off the alarm.

10. Don't talk with anyone **who** you think might be connected with the competition.

11. **Who** had my job before me?

12. It was she **whom** they selected for the Cabinet post.

13. Sometimes it is the one **who** does the most work who is the least tired.

14. We plan to hire an assistant **who** is a good proofreader.

15. The prize will be given to **whoever** writes the best essay.

16. The bookkeeper is the one to **whom** the figures should be mailed.

17. Give the recipe for the vegetarian chili to **whoever** calls for it.

18. **Whom** did you really want to be there?

19. She is the contestant **whom** they sent to us.

20. This vacation spot will refresh **whoever** seeks refuge here.

Who, Whom, That, Which Quiz 1 Answers

1. Ahmed is the skydiver **who** broke his back last week.

2. That is a problem **that** can't be solved without a calculator. (CORRECT)
    OR That is a problem **which** can't be solved without a calculator.

3. That is a promise **which** cannot be broken. (CORRECT) **OR** That is a
    promise **that** cannot be broken.

4. The domino theory, **which** stated that, when one country fell to
    Communism, others in the area would likely fall, was used as an
    argument to continue the Vietnam War.

5. The game **that** intrigues Gretchen the most is dominoes.

6. Gandhi, **who** was a role model for nonviolence to millions, was
    assassinated. (CORRECT)

7. The tomatoes **that** grow in her garden are unlike those you buy in a
    store.

8. The tomatoes from her garden, **which** grew larger than those in the
    grocery store, were sweet and ripe. (CORRECT)

9. The baker **who** baked that bread should win an award.

Who, Whom, That, Which Quiz 2 Answers

1. Books have been written **that** address the horrors of the Salem witch
    trials.

2. That book, **which** was discovered in the basement of the library, will
    be published next year.

3. That is a book **which** I have not yet read. (CORRECT)

4. The state law **that** banned logging ancient redwoods was put on the
    ballot by voter initiative.

5. The campaign to protect ancient redwoods, **which** began at the
    grassroots level, has gained the attention of lawmakers at the national
    level. (CORRECT)

6. The wheelchairs in that corner, **which** are motorized, are helpful to
    those who live in urban areas. (CORRECT)

7. The people **who** are on my list haven't shown up yet.

8. The couple, **who** are my parents, left the party an hour ago.

9. Officer, he is the one **who** stole my purse.

Adjectives and Adverbs <u>Quiz 1 Answers</u>

1. Come **quickly** or we will miss our bus.

2. You drive so **slowly** that I am afraid someone will hit the car from behind.

3. I have never been **more sure** of anything in my life. (**OR** *surer*)

4. Ella was the **better** of the two sisters at gymnastics.

5. You did that somersault so **well**.

6. Rochelle felt **bad** about forgetting Devlin's birthday.

7. This is the **worst** oil spill I have ever seen. (CORRECT)

8. The jasmine has bloomed and smells very **sweet**. (CORRECT)

9. You look **angry**. What did I do?

10. She looked **suspiciously** at the man wearing the trench coat. (CORRECT)

11. **This** tree looks as though it is infested with beetles.

12. **Those** bushes need to be trimmed. (CORRECT)

13. When was the last time you had no allergy symptoms and felt **well**?

14. In the library, you have to be **quieter than** when you are outside.

15. She felt **good** about getting her puppy from the SPCA. (CORRECT)

16. Charlotte has a **better** approach to solving that problem.

17. Which is **worse**, a toothache or a headache?

18. She reacted **swiftly**, which made him feel **bad** about insulting her.

19. The herbs in the salad tasted **bitter**. (CORRECT)

20. Sharon fought **bitterly** against her ex-husband for custody of their daughter. (CORRECT)

Adjectives and Adverbs <u>Quiz 2 Answers</u>

1. We are **really** happy to be of service to you and your family. (**OR** *very*)

2. The perfume smells **sweet**.

3. I feel **bad** about what happened. (CORRECT)

4. Of all the holidays, this is the **most** joyful. (CORRECT)

5. This wine tastes **dry** to me.

6. Don't feel too **bad** about what you said.

7. This leotard hugs me **firmly**. (CORRECT)

8. Life in the city is exciting, but life in the country is **better**.

9. If you don't speak **clearly**, the audience will not understand you.

10. The **sweet** smell of roses has no match. (CORRECT)

11. Walk **slowly** or you will be sorry.

12. You don't look as though you feel **well** today. (CORRECT)

13. You don't look as though you are doing **well** today. (CORRECT)

14. My son doesn't feel very **well** today.

15. She was the **more** beautiful of the two.

16. The dentist said, "I will be finished drilling **really** soon." (**OR** *very*)

17. Speak **slowly** or you will lose your audience. (**OR** *more slowly*)

18. Juanita said she had better memories of Paris **than** of Rome.

19. If you won't tell me your secret now, **then** when will you tell me?

20. I would rather have hope **than** hold despair. (CORRECT)

Problems with Prepositions <u>Quiz 1 Answers</u>

1. Our ship leaves **on** August 15.

2. I could **have** danced all night.

3. Where did you get this?

4. If we split it evenly **among** the three of us, no one will be unhappy.

5. You can't just walk **into** the house without knocking.

6. He will be back **on** the tenth.

7. Take your plate off the table.

8. Cut the pie into six slices.

9. **As** the invitation stated, we'll see you **on** the tenth for our reunion.

10. I don't know what you are talking about. (CORRECT)

11. You could **have** told me about the mistake earlier.

12. I don't know where he is or I would tell you.

Problems with Prepositions <u>Quiz 2 Answers</u>

1. Tell me where you found this.

2. Sami will meet him **on** May 18 at the Washington Hotel in downtown Seattle.

3. I should **have** known he would steal money from my purse.

4. We hiked into the woods and fell off a log while crossing a creek.

5. That lie is still coming between the two of them. (CORRECT)

6. **As** I said, I am sorry for the muddy print her paws left on the carpet.

7. I should **have** wiped her paws first.

8. The robbery happened just **as** you said it did.

9. She is the most enthusiastic student a teacher could hope for. (CORRECT)

10. His brother's birthday is **on** June 14.

11. Please take off your shoes when you come **inside**.

12. Where did she go?

Affect vs. Effect <u>Quiz 1 Answers</u>

1. The **effect** of the antibiotic on her infection was surprising.

2. I did not know that antibiotics could **affect** people so quickly.

3. Plastic surgery had an **effect**, not only on her appearance, but on her self-esteem.

4. If the chemotherapy has no **effect**, should she get surgery for the tumor?

5. When will we know if the chemotherapy has taken **effect**?

6. Losing her hair from chemotherapy did not **affect** her as much as her friends had expected.

7. We cannot **effect** a new policy without the board of directors voting on it first.

8. To be an **effective** leader, you should know both your strengths as well as your weaknesses.

9. The movie *Winged Migration* had two **effects** on him: He became an environmental advocate and a bird lover.

10. The net **effect** of blowing the whistle on her boss was that she was eventually given his position.

11. What was the **effect** of his promotion?

12. His decision **affected** everyone here.

13. We had to **effect** a reduction in costs.

14. The critics greatly **affected** his thinking.

15. How were you able to **effect** such radical changes?

16. That book had a major **effect** on his philosophy.

Affect vs. Effect <u>Quiz 2 Answers</u>

1. Shelley had to **effect** great reductions in her expenses.

2. What do you suppose the **effect** of her resignation will be?

3. The changes had an enormous **effect** on production.

4. The crisis has greatly **affected** our lifestyle.

5. They were able to **effect** an increase in their savings.

6. Roberta has **effected** many improvements in office procedures.

7. The rainy weather had a bad **effect** on attendance at the seminar.

8. The new personnel ruling does not **affect** my status.

9. The new director will reorganize the office and **effect** a number of changes in personnel.

10. What she said had no **effect** on the boss.

11. I don't know why the cold air **affects** my skin.

12. I hope to **effect** improvements in my work.

13. The knowledge I gain from this course will **affect** my performance.

14. The new schedule will take **effect** in October.

15. The supervisor **effected** a reconciliation between Donya and Dayne.

16. The new law goes into **effect** tomorrow.

Lay vs. Lie <u>Quiz 1 Answers</u>

1. I am dizzy and need to **lie** down.

2. When I got dizzy yesterday, I **lay** down.

3. My brother **lays** carpet for a living. (CORRECT)

4. **Lay** the carpet after painting the walls. (CORRECT)

5. We need to **lay** this baby down for a nap.

6. We will know when we have **laid** this issue to rest when we no longer fight about it.

7. The lions are **lying** in wait for their prey.

8. The lions have **lain** in wait for their prey.

9. I **laid** the blanket over her as she slept. (CORRECT)

10. I will **lay** my head on my pillow shortly.

Lay vs. Lie Quiz 2 Answers

1. **Lie** down next to me and I will hold you.

2. When my dog is tired, she **lies** on her back.

3. I think we can **lay** the groundwork for lasting changes within the organization. (CORRECT)

4. I have **lain** down because of a headache every afternoon this week.

5. Henry has **lied** consistently on the witness stand. (CORRECT)

6. Sandra has **laid** out her plan for reorganization.

7. The preschoolers have **lain** down after lunch each day. (CORRECT)

8. After I took the pill, I had to **lie** down.

9. I have **laid** my cards on the table. (CORRECT)

10. **Lie** on this lounge chair and soak up some sun.

Advice vs. Advise Quiz 1 Answers

1. Adele is always happy to offer **advice** if you ask her for it.

2. The lawyer **advised** him to plead guilty.

3. If you want to go on the senior trip, I would strongly **advise** you to start saving your money.

4. Our new members are impressed with the level of **advice** they received from the leadership group.

5. Sara always takes my **advice** to heart.

6. I'd like to ask an engineer to **advise** us on the design.

7. We **advised** the city council that the deadline was tentative and might need to be extended.

8. Lakeisha knows she can always go to her best friend for **advice**.

9. Don't give **advice** that you're not willing to follow yourself.

10. Randall has a bad habit of offering unsolicited **advice**.

Advice vs. Advise Quiz 2 Answers

1. You can offer me **advice**, but that doesn't mean I will follow it.

2. Paolo will give **advice** to anyone, including complete strangers.

3. Next time I need financial **advice**, I think I'll call Jerome.

4. From the beginning, she **advised** me that the project would require fast turnaround times.

5. It's essential that we find a professional to **advise** us on this situation.

6. I'm sure that Adriana will give careful consideration to your **advice**.

7. It's important to interact with others in your industry to exchange ideas and **advice**.

8. I strongly **advise** you to call your doctor immediately.

9. The policeman **advised** him of his rights while placing the handcuffs around his wrists.

10. Mark won't mind if you call to ask his **advice** about this.

Their vs. There vs. They're Quiz 1 Answers

1. According to an old legend, **there** is treasure buried on that island.

2. Juan and Pancho just called to let us know **they're** coming for dinner.

3. **There** is a mouse in my closet!

4. I can't wait to see the looks on **their** faces when I tell them the truth.

5. I wonder if **they're** planning to go shopping with us.

6. The children went upstairs to play after clearing **their** plates at dinner.

7. It's **their** decision, so I'll just stay out of it.

8. I don't know what **they're** doing to cause all that noise, but it's giving me a headache!

9. The kids haven't called yet; I'm concerned about **their** being out so late at night.

10. I believe Wynona left her glasses over **there**.

Their vs. There vs. They're Quiz 2 Answers

1. Do you see the bird's nest over **there**?

2. I don't appreciate **their** ignoring me when I speak to them.

3. I'm not sure where **they're** planning to hold the company picnic this year.

4. It's **their** truck; I'm just borrowing it for the day.

5. The students were instructed to put down **their** pencils after finishing the exam.

6. **They're** baking the turkey for tonight's dinner.

7. You should have seen the shock in **their** eyes when I won the award.

8. **There** is a telephone down the hall.

9. Have Paige and Preston called to say whether **they're** going to the school play?

10. I was told that **there** would be a free breakfast this morning.

More Confusing Words and Homonyms Quiz 1 Answers

1. Many people don't stop to consider how current events affect their **everyday** lives.

2. I hope the solar **flare** doesn't affect our computer equipment.

3. It's amazing that **hangars** can be built large enough to accommodate today's gigantic airplanes.

4. We'll need a forklift to place all those boxes on the **pallet**.

5. Would you like to have a sneak **peek** at the restaurant before it opens?

6. Use the **reins** to guide the horse along the path.

7. The company will have to **raise** adequate funds before it can move forward with the project.

8. My grandmother taught me how to **sew** when I was a little girl.

9. Have you ever watched someone **shear** a sheep?

10. I'd like to go to the state fair on **Sunday**.

11. If you ask her, Katerina will admit that she's quite **vain**.

12. We'll need to have a custom **yoke** built for the oxen.

13. Everyone is planning to go on the trip **except** Dolores.

14. We are **all ready** for summer vacation.

15. Some religious leaders burn incense at an **altar** as a form of prayer.

16. It will be easier to move the cabinet if you hold it at the **base**.

17. If you ever come in contact with a wild **boar**, do not provoke it.

18. Please be careful not to **break** the vase.

19. **Canvas** fabric is known for its durability, so I'd recommend using it for your project.

20. She ate the **carrot** raw.

More Confusing Words and Homonyms Quiz 2 Answers

1. He used the information from several of Heidi's newsletters, but he didn't **cite** his sources.

2. She wasn't interested in being part of any of the **cliques** at school.

3. We have different specialties, so our business services **complement** one another.

4. I'm planning to have the chocolate cake for **dessert**.

5. Many countries use questionable techniques to **elicit** information from their prisoners.

6. Carlos can't wait to go to the **fair** this weekend.

7. We hired professionals to clean out our chimney **flue**.

8. After screaming at the concert, Kamilah's voice was **hoarse**.

9. The bolt of **lightning** struck the house and started a fire.

10. These pants are **loose**, so I must have lost weight.

11. You know better than to **meddle** in other people's business.

12. I would like a chocolate **mousse** cake for my birthday.

13. Armando left the other **oar** in the canoe.

14. Casey looked **pale**, so I thought she might be sick.

15. Having life insurance gives us **peace** of mind.

16. Before hanging the wallpaper, check to see if the walls are **plumb**.

17. We couldn't believe the squirrel climbed up that **pole**.

18. When we opened the trash can, it **reeked** of rotten meat.

19. Obtaining a driver's license is often considered a **rite** of passage.

20. When Marie's plane hadn't arrived, her mother started **wringing** her hands in worry.

More Confusing Words and Homonyms Quiz 3 Answers

1. The magician impressed the audience with his **sleight** of hand.

2. Connie ordered her business **stationery** from the local print shop.

3. Dominic **threw** the garbage bag into the dumpster.

4. Even though Kurt asked my opinion, he didn't want to listen to my **advice**.

5. **Whose** job is it to clean the kitchen tonight?

6. Until Simon called, I had almost given up on this deal **altogether**.

7. A few days ago, Taya called to request my **assistance** with her latest project.

8. Many people are hesitant to **bare** their souls on the Internet.

9. Students have a hard time remembering that the **capital** of California is Sacramento.

10. One day I'd like to go scuba diving and photograph the **coral** reefs.

11. When you sand any wood surface, always start with **coarse** sandpaper.

12. I wasn't at all surprised when Cindy decided to join the U.S. Marine **Corps**.

13. Every time I try to sneak up on you, the floor **creaks**.

14. Please let Ricardo know when you're done with that project so you're not just sitting there **idle**.

15. **Regardless** of Anita's recent illness, she still maintains a positive attitude.

16. Juanita **led** the policemen to the place where she had parked her car.

17. If you'll give me a knife, I'll **pare** the apple.

18. Denise isn't known for her **patience** with children.

19. There's an open market outside of town where merchants can **peddle** their goods.

20. This is the fifth time that Josef has been called to the **principal's** office.

Effective Writing Quiz 1 Answers

1. We are no longer able to reconcile; therefore, attorneys will be used to effect the dissolution of our marriage.
   We have hired attorneys to help us with our divorce.

2. The weather had adverse impacts on our boat resulting in the necessity to rescue us from the water.
   Our boat capsized in the storm so we needed rescuing.

3. The leak in the bottom of the boat was due to poor maintenance on the part of the crew.
   The crew did not maintain the boat so the bottom leaked.

4. Our marriage ended in a divorce.
   We divorced. **OR** *We ended our marriage.*

5. The boy was struck in the face by the pie as it flew from the girl's hand.
   The girl threw the pie and it hit the boy's face.

6. It was not likely that no one would want to claim ownership of the new sports car.
   Someone will most likely want to claim ownership of the new sports car.

7. There are many ideas that are worth exploring by us at this meeting.
   Let's explore the many worthwhile ideas at this meeting.

8. Martin could not find time to work, shop, and go for walks with the dogs.
   Martin could not find time to work, shop, and walk the dogs.

9. Jordan did not believe that Serena had embarrassed him unintentionally.
   Jordan believed that Serena had embarrassed him intentionally.

10. It is a shame that there are so many holidays that go uncelebrated.
    It is a shame that so many holidays go uncelebrated. **OR** *I wish we celebrated more holidays.*

11. While singing in the shower, the bar of soap slipped from her hands.
    The bar of soap slipped from her hands while she sang in the shower.

12. Looking back, the dog was following us.
    When we looked back, we saw the dog following us.

13. Lying on a stretcher, they carried him out.
    He was carried out on a stretcher.

14. Flying out the window, he grabbed the papers.
    He grabbed the papers as they were flying out the window.

15. Stepping off the bus, the shopping center was just ahead.
    As I stepped off the bus, I saw the shopping center just ahead.

Effective Writing Quiz 2 Answers

1. It is necessary that you not be uninformed about this case.
   You must be informed about this case.

2. There is ample evidence which indicates that the attorneys for the defense did not provide inadequate counseling to their client.
   Ample evidence shows that the defense attorneys provided adequate counseling to their client.

3. Speaking and to listen well are important elements of communication.
   Speaking and listening well are important elements of communication. **OR**
   To speak and to listen well are important communication elements.

4. To win is the obvious goal, but playing fair is important too.
   Winning is the obvious goal, but playing fair is important too. **OR**
   To win is the obvious goal, but to play fair is important too.

5. They were charged with assault, robbery, and forging checks.
   They were charged with assault, robbery, and check forgery.

6. I remember his generosity and that he was considerate.
   I remember his generosity and consideration.

7. She worked quickly and in an efficient manner.
   She worked quickly and efficiently.

8. When working with power tools, eyes should be protected.
   When working with power tools, protect your eyes. **OR**
   Protect your eyes when you use power tools.

9. When changing a diaper, a baby should be on his or her back.
   When changing a diaper, lay a baby down on his or her back. **OR**
   Lay a baby down on his or her back when changing a diaper.

10. I have some letters the mail carrier delivered in my purse.
    The mail carrier delivered some letters that I have in my purse.

11. We have tuna casserole I made in the refrigerator.
    In the refrigerator, we have tuna casserole that I made.

12. Mollie came over while I was playing the piano with a piece of pound cake.
    While I was playing the piano, Mollie came over with a piece of pound cake.

13. While asleep, the flea bit the dog.
    The flea bit the sleeping dog.

14. I tried calling to tell you about that TV show five times.
    I called five times to tell you about that TV show.

15. Although very spicy, Dana managed to finish the enchilada.
    Dana managed to finish the enchilada although it was very spicy.

Grammar Mastery Test Answers

1. Some of the desserts **were** left by the end of the birthday party.

2. The papa bear thought that some of his porridge **was** missing.

3. Your brilliant excuses almost **make** up for your tardiness.

4. Neither Jackson nor Jenna **is** playing hooky. (CORRECT)

5. Neither Jackson nor I **am** playing hooky.

6. Either of us **is** capable of winning. (CORRECT)

7. All of the class **is** willing to take part in the prank. (CORRECT)

8. One-third of the eligible population **tends** not to vote in national elections.

9. One-third of the voters **tend** not to cast their ballots in national elections.

10. Here **are** the paper clips you requested.

11. She is one of those doctors who **make** house calls. (CORRECT)

12. Dr. Cresta is one of those professors who **do** whatever it takes to get **their** point across to **their** students.

13. She is the only professor who **does** what it takes to help her students learn joyfully. (CORRECT)

14. **She** and **he** are always fighting.

15. When Toni and **he** come over, we always have a great time.

16. It is **we** who must decide whether to tax ourselves or cut spending. (CORRECT)

17. Between you and **me**, this class is a joke.

18. **Who** do you think you are to give me advice about dating? (CORRECT)

19. **Who** makes up these English rules anyway? (CORRECT)

20. **Who** do you think should win?

21. **Whom** are you voting for?

22. **Whoever** has the keys gets to be in the driver's seat. (CORRECT)

23. We are willing to work with **whomever** you recommend.

24. The thoughts **that** Ted presented at the meeting were so worthwhile. (CORRECT)

25. The thoughts that Ted presented, **which** were about shifting national priorities, were well received.

26. When you do a job so **well**, you can expect a raise.

27. Bonnie was a **good** sport about losing the race. (CORRECT)

28. Harry smells **good**. What is the aftershave he is wearing? (CORRECT)

29. Lisa did so **well** on the test that she was allowed to accelerate to the next level. (CORRECT)

30. Our puppy is definitely **sweeter** than her brother.

31. With triplets, I have to be careful to divide everything equally **among** them or they will fight.

32. Karen should **have** known that her cheap umbrella would break in the storm.

33. Sometimes the **effects** of our generosity may seem minimal, but our good intentions do make a difference. (CORRECT)

34. Ben thought he had **laid** my jacket on that bench.

35. Our company policy will not allow me to **accept** a gift worth more than $50.

36. They thought we were late, but my wife and I were **already** at the restaurant.

37. **Regardless** of who was there first, we were all very hungry and ready to eat.

38. We could hardly believe that the Giants could **lose** the game by that many runs.

39. Isn't it amazing how long that mime can remain completely **stationary**? (CORRECT)

40. The department's **principal** concern is the safety of all employees. (CORRECT)

41. How did they manage to serve cold ice cream in the middle of the vast **desert**?

42. The boss complimented Ari on his excellent presentation. (CORRECT)

43. The judge did not believe any of **their** stories.

44. Ilana said she wanted to become **an** FBI agent when she grew up.

45. The meeting attendees were to express a preference **among** five cleanup plans.

46. To be a good billiards player, you've got to think **further** ahead than just the next shot.

47. Paul should **have** known better than to act like that.

48. The golf course at the resort is lovely, but I prefer **its** swimming pool.

49. I paid the cab fare and Alejandro paid for dinner. (CORRECT)

50. Marta completed five **fewer** problems than I did in the same amount of time.

Punctuation, Capitalization, and Writing Numbers Pretest Answers

1. Go **west** three blocks and turn right.

2. Yes, sir, I will do it immediately.

3. "How," I asked, "**can** you always be so forgetful?"

4. The woman who is standing there is his ex-wife.

5. Although we have a competent staff, bottlenecks do occur.

6. I did not receive the order; therefore, I will not pay my bill. (CORRECT)

7. We offer a variety of drinks, for instance, beer. (CORRECT. Comma after *instance* is optional.)

8. Is that book **yours**?

9. We have much to do; for example, the carpets need vacuuming.

10. Estimates for the work have been forwarded, and a breakdown of costs has been included. (CORRECT)

11. Because of his embezzling, the company went bankrupt.

12. A proposal that makes harassment of whales illegal has just passed. (CORRECT)

13. You may, of course, call us anytime you wish.

14. Paolo hurried to the depot to meet his aunt and two cousins.

15. Finish your job; it is imperative that you do.

16. Sofia and Aidan's house was recently painted. (CORRECT)

17. "Stop it!" I said. "Don't ever do that again."

18. I would, therefore, like to have an explanation for the missing cash.

19. "Would you like to accompany me?" he asked.

20. I have always had a mental block against **math**.

21. He is a strong, healthy man.

22. To apply for this job, you must have previous experience.

23. Marge, the woman with blonde hair, will be our speaker this evening.

24. He thought quickly and then answered the question in complete detail.

25. He asked if he could be excused.

26. It is hailing, not raining.

27. We will grant you immunity if you decide to cooperate with us.

28. You signed the contract; consequently, you must provide us with the raw materials.

29. I would like, however, to read the fine print first.

30. You are required to bring the following: **sleeping** bag, food, and a sewing kit.

31. The three **companies'** computers were stolen.

32. The **women's** department is upstairs and to your left.

33. It hurt **its** paw.

34. One of the **lawyers** left her briefcase.

35. "What does it take to become a licensed architect?" she asked.

36. I can't remember if her birthday falls on a Saturday, Sunday, or Monday next year.

37. I need to locate four states on the map: Arkansas, Ohio, Illinois, and Utah.

38. The email read, "Hi, Camille. I haven't heard from you in two weeks."

39. The veterinarian said, "Unless **it's** bleeding and doesn't stop, don't worry about it."

40. In letting go of needing to discuss this with her mother anymore, Wendy declared, "This is her karma, not mine."

41. You must study hard to get good grades at a major university.

42. **One-fourth** of the police force voted for a pay raise.

43. Whether Bella has five students or fifteen students, she will give the test. (CORRECT) **OR** Whether Bella has **5** students or **15** students, she will give the test.

44. I owe you **$15**, not $16. **OR** I owe you $15.00, not **$16.00**.

Commas <u>Quiz 1</u> Answers

1. I took Angie, the one with the freckles, to the movie last night.

2. Jeremy and I have had our share of arguments.

3. You are, I am sure, telling the truth.

4. She left Albany, New York on January 18 of that year. (CORRECT. Comma after *New York* is optional.)

5. I need sugar, butter, and eggs from the grocery store.

6. Please, Sasha, come home as soon as you can.

7. Although you may be right, I cannot take your word for it.

8. We will grant you immunity if you decide to cooperate with us. (CORRECT)

9. I am typing a letter and she is talking on the phone. (CORRECT. Comma after *letter* is optional.)

10. She finished her work and then took a long lunch.

11. Mae said, "Why don't you come up and see me sometime?"

12. You said that I could go, didn't you? (CORRECT)

13. To apply for this job, you must have a Social Security card.

14. He seems to be such a lonely, quiet man, doesn't he?

15. She wore a brightly colored dress. (CORRECT)

16. She has a good, healthy attitude about her work.

Commas <u>Quiz 2</u> Answers

1. Girls who have red hair are very lucky.

2. He asked where his hat was. (CORRECT)

3. They are, one might say, true believers. (CORRECT)

4. Cheryl arrived in Denver, Colorado, hoping to find a good job. (Comma after *Colorado* is optional.)

5. On July 20, 1969, astronauts landed on the moon for the first time.

6. Life, liberty, and the pursuit of happiness are three guarantees granted to us by our forefathers.

7. I told you, Jesse, never to ask me that question again.

8. I may as well not speak if you refuse to even listen. (CORRECT)

9. I am already finished cooking, but he has not taken his shower yet.

10. I walked all the way to the bus stop and waited for a bus for over an hour. (CORRECT)

11. It is drizzling, not pouring.

12. What a delicious, appetizing meal! (CORRECT)

13. Dario drove to the airport to meet his wife and children. (CORRECT)

14. Yes, I can be ready in five minutes.

15. I will not stop you if you want to leave.

16. Rosie Hernandez, Ph.D., will be our guest speaker.

Semicolons and Colons Quiz 1 Answers

1. You asked for forgiveness; he granted it to you.

2. We ask, therefore, that you keep this matter confidential.

3. The order was requested six weeks ago; therefore, I expected the shipment to arrive by now.

4. The American flag has three colors, namely, red, white, and blue. (CORRECT. Comma before *namely* may be a semicolon.)

5. Clothes are often made from synthetic material, for instance, rayon.

6. If you believe in magic, magical things will happen; but if you do not believe in magic, you will discover nothing to be magical.

7. The orchestra, excluding the violin section, was not up to par.

8. I have been to San Francisco, California; Reno, Nevada; and Seattle, Washington.

9. I need a few items at the store: clothespins, a bottle opener, and napkins.

10. I answered the phone, but no one seemed to be on the other end of the line. (Comma is optional.)

11. I wanted a cup of coffee, not a glass of milk. (CORRECT)

12. You have won the following prizes, namely, a car, a trip to Hawaii, and a bathrobe. (Comma before *namely* may be a semicolon.)

13. If you can possibly arrange it, please visit us; but if you cannot, let us know.

14. I gave her a lot of money while we were married; hence, I do not wish to pay her a dime in alimony.

15. We have a variety of desserts, for instance, apple pie. (CORRECT. Comma after *instance* is optional.)

16. I needed only three cards to win, namely, the ten of hearts, the jack of diamonds, and the king of hearts. (Comma before *namely* may be a semicolon.)

17. I needed only three cards to win: the ten of hearts, the jack of diamonds, and the king of hearts.

18. I would, therefore, like to have an explanation for the missing cash.

19. Nature lovers will appreciate seeing whales, sea lions, and pelicans.

20. He has friends from Iowa and Nebraska, and Illinois is his home state.

21. We have set this restriction: do your homework before watching television.

Semicolons and Colons <u>Quiz 2 Answers</u>

1. He has friends from Montana, Iowa, and Nebraska; and Illinois is his home state.

2. This is a difficult exercise but I am having fun. (CORRECT. Comma after *exercise* is optional.)

3. Although this is a difficult exercise, I am having fun.

4. This is a difficult exercise; I am having fun though.

5. The man who is wearing dark glasses is an FBI undercover agent. (CORRECT)

6. That FBI agent, who is wearing dark glasses, once protected the president.

7. Did you, John, eat my cake?

8. Did John eat my cake? (CORRECT)

9. Did his friend John eat my cake? (CORRECT)

10. Did John, his friend, eat the cake?

11. If everything goes according to plan, he will retire at 40; if real estate prices continue to drop, however, he may have to work until he is 65.

12. Golden retrievers, which are known to be gentle, are also loyal.

13. Dogs that are gentle are often good family pets. (CORRECT)

14. I would love to be rich and famous although fame has mixed blessings. (CORRECT)

15. I would love to be rich and famous, and famous is the first priority.

16. She chose the field of journalism because of Nellie Bly, the first woman reporter.

17. They built an adobe house but then they decided to move. (CORRECT. Comma after *house* is optional.)

18. They built an adobe house but then decided to move. (CORRECT)

19. They built an adobe house; however, they decided to move.

20. They built an adobe house because they decided never to move again. (CORRECT)

21. Since they moved to the desert, they decided to build an adobe house.

22. Mr. Liu held this belief: if he worked hard, he would be able to save enough money to travel to Madagascar and photograph rarely seen animals.

Question Marks, Quotation Marks, and Parentheses
Quiz 1 Answers

1. He wanted to know when you will be here.

2. "Well," she said, "you certainly didn't waste any time."

3. "Is it almost over?" he asked.

4. "I've had it up to here!" she screamed.

5. The song asks, "Would you like to swing on a star?"

6. Carmen said, "She said, 'I'll never leave you.'"

7. She requested (actually she pleaded) that her name be withheld. (**OR** use commas instead of parentheses.)

8. This contract guarantees that we will (1.) deliver the merchandise, (2.) pay for all damaged goods, and (3.) make you the exclusive carrier of our products. (**OR** just use parentheses around the numbers)

9. "May I have a rain check on that lunch?" I asked.

10. Do you believe the saying, "It is better to vote for what you want and not get it than to vote for what you don't want and get it"?

11. Bernard said, "Waldo asked, 'Who took my pencil sharpener?'"

12. "May I see your I.D. card?" the clerk asked.

Question Marks, Quotation Marks, and Parentheses
Quiz 2 Answers

1. "Correct me if I am wrong," she said.

2. "Correct me if I am wrong," she said, "but don't you usually drive a truck?"

3. Sandi asked, "Did Jeri say, 'I am pregnant'?"

4. I can have lunch with you tomorrow (Friday).

5. I hope you are feeling better. (I am sick today.)

6. Did he ask, "Where are my keys?"

7. Harry needs to know if he can count on you.

8. I smiled (actually I laughed) when I saw the expression on his face. (CORRECT **OR** you may use a pair of em dashes or commas)

9. Nicole said with shock in her voice, "I can't believe what I just saw!"

10. It wouldn't surprise me if he quit his job.

11. I can't think of what to say.

12. Tessa thinks he said that he would go to the movie with her.

Apostrophes Quiz 1 Answers

1. Her husband's wallet was full of curious, little items.

2. I went to my mother-in-law's house for dinner last night.

3. You may not enter Mr. Harris's office without his permission.

4. The girl's vitality and humor were infectious. [one girl]

5. The women's dresses are on the second floor.

6. It's a shame that had to happen.

7. It's hard to believe that winter is almost here.

8. Her mother and father's business went bankrupt.

9. It is his word against mine.

10. The actresses' costumes looked beautiful on them.

11. Sharon's arriving was unexpected.

12. The movie had its desired effect.

Apostrophes Quiz 2 Answers

1. His 6s and 8s looked alike.

2. Where would I find the men's room?

3. Both secretaries' vacations caused a delay in output.

4. New clients' accounts showed an 11 percent increase in sales. (*clients* is plural)

5. Most children's imaginations run wild when told that story.

6. Both sons-in-law's opinions were considered.

7. Several M.D.s agreed that one bacterial strain caused many of the symptoms.

8. These M.D.s' credentials are excellent.

9. Both brothers-in-law's jobs required physical labor.

10. Do you mind my looking at the earrings in this jewelry case?

11. Your right to privacy will not be abused.

12. Its beauty is unsurpassed.

Hyphens Between Words Quiz 1 Answers

1. She jumped from a two-story building.

2. The show's cancellation was a real letdown. (CORRECT)

3. You must let down your guard.

4. You certainly have a go-get-it nature.

5. What a cute little bird she has! (CORRECT)

6. We offer around-the-clock coverage.

7. Look left and right before you cross the street.

8. The left-handed pitcher threw fastballs at almost 100 miles per hour.

9. The delicious, gooey frosting melted before we could refrigerate the cake.

10. Do you remember anything you read in the fourth grade? (CORRECT)

11. This is seventh-grade reading material.

12. Beware of high-pressure telemarketers. (CORRECT)

Hyphens Between Words **Quiz 2 Answers**

1. Turn left after the big red door. (CORRECT)

2. This is a one-family dwelling.

3. Do you think he has above-average intelligence?

4. I would like that antique picture frame. (CORRECT)

5. She owns income-producing property.

6. That is a well-written letter.

7. If you are not satisfied, we will give you your money back.

8. This product comes with a money-back guarantee.

9. The highway patrol will crack down on drunk drivers over the Memorial Day holiday.

10. Please let up on your criticisms about my writing.

11. Paying a $100 fine for a speeding ticket was a wake-up call.

12. The small plastic lid seems to be missing.

Hyphens with -ly Words **Quiz 1 Answers**

1. This appears to be a firmly built house. (CORRECT)

2. A dimly lit restaurant can be rather romantic. (CORRECT)

3. A friendly little dog is all I need for company. (CORRECT)

4. The data was readily available. (CORRECT)

5. He is a happily married man. (CORRECT)

6. What kindly-looking eyes my grandfather had.

7. If someone causes bodily harm while defending herself, should she be prosecuted?

8. The tree was firmly planted in the ground.

9. Noah's art work is positively beautiful. (CORRECT)

10. Your award is richly deserved.

Hyphens with -ly Words Quiz 2 Answers

1. You are certainly a likely-looking prospect for the job.
2. A silly-acting child is a joy to behold.
3. A chilly, snowy morning would be a refreshing sight.
4. The lovely-sounding music came from that singer over there.
5. The friendly-acting dog growled whenever he had a bone nearby.
6. She appears to be happily married. (CORRECT)
7. The smelly, dirty dog shook the water off itself.
8. The scantily clad doll was pulled from the toy store's inventory. (CORRECT)
9. Ella showed her carefully prepared report to her supervisor.
10. Boris's goals are poorly defined. (CORRECT)

Hyphens with Prefixes Quiz 1 Answers

1. antiaircraft
2. ultra-anxious
3. antidepressant
4. antifreeze
5. anti-impressionism
6. unpatriotic
7. nonprofessional
8. nonexistent
9. self-paced
10. cooperation

Hyphens with Prefixes Quiz 2 Answers

1. non-Jewish
2. preexisting
3. reestablish
4. self-satisfied

5. ex-Marine

6. anti-inflammatory

7. antiwar

8. unnatural

9. nonessential

10. biennial

Hyphens with re- Words Quiz 1 Answers

1. When can we refurnish our home?

2. Our friendship was renewed.

3. I cannot recollect the story.

4. Please re-collect the papers, Mikaela.

5. That point should be reemphasized.

6. I enjoy re-covering chairs.

7. Because of new DNA evidence, the police need to re-solve the case.

8. I resent your questioning my integrity.

9. Please re-sign the documents you signed yesterday.

10. It takes a lot of resolve to eat nutritiously.

Hyphens with re- Words Quiz 2 Answers

1. The astronauts began the reentry phase.

2. Martin Luther began the Reformation.

3. I made a mistake and had to re-form the clay.

4. I must re-press the wrinkled suit.

5. I will re-lease the apartment after the current tenants leave. (lease again)

6. The couple was reunited after a long separation.

7. It is not unusual to repress traumatic memories.

8. If he doesn't re-press his slacks after unpacking, they will be rumpled.

9. Would you vote to reelect Senator Hogan?

10. His reserved nature is often mistaken for aloofness.

Capitalization Quiz 1 Answers

1. She said, "Bees are not the only insects that sting."

2. "You must understand," he pleaded, "that I need more time to pay you."

3. Mark Paxton, the vice president of the company, embezzled over one million dollars.

4. The president of the United States wields much power.

5. I live in the northeastern part of the state where the climate is colder. (CORRECT)

6. The West, especially California, is famous for its cutting-edge technology. (CORRECT)

7. Have you read *All the King's Men?*

8. I enjoy summer more than any other season.

9. Employees of the company were laid off with little hope of returning to work.

10. My dear Mr. Simpson:

11. Sincerely yours,

Capitalization Quiz 2 Answers

1. I lived on Elm Street a few years ago.

2. The American River is extremely cold all year.

3. Do not swim in that river because of the swift current.

4. "You must realize," he explained, "that my circumstances are desperate." (CORRECT)

5. "Stop it!" she screamed. "Don't ever do that again."

6. She said, "We strive hard for a better world, but we don't lift a finger for perfection."

7. The West has a milder climate than the East.

8. You must take the following courses: history, geometry, and French.

9. The supervisor will decide whether state regulations prohibit our taking Monday as a holiday. (CORRECT)

10. My major requires that I take Calculus 1, history, and French.

11. The Federal Reserve Board will raise interest rates over many state agencies' objections.

Writing Numbers Quiz 1 Answers

1. I asked for **two** copies each for my **12** employees.

2. If only 14 people show up, will you still make a speech? (CORRECT) **OR** If only **fourteen** people show up, will you still make the speech?

3. **One-fifth** of the inventory was ruined in the fire.

4. A **two-thirds** majority is needed to pass the measure.

5. The tree grew only **0.5** of an inch because of the drought.

6. He hit more home runs in '06 than in '05. (CORRECT)

7. Her earnings rose from $500 to **$5,000** in one year because of her marketing efforts.

8. We didn't get to bed until **eleven thirty** last night.

9. At exactly 11:33, the phone rang. (CORRECT)

10. **Forty-seven** people were hired last month.

Writing Numbers Quiz 2 Answers

1. If you let her nap for 2 hours, she will be up until midnight. (CORRECT) **OR** If you let her nap for **two** hours, she will be up until midnight.

2. His company grew from seven employees to thirty-seven employees in 4 months. (CORRECT) **OR** His company grew from **7** employees to **37** employees in four months.

3. A **0.9%** profit is not the same as a **9.0%** profit.

4. The hotel woke us up at **six** o'clock.

5. A 7:40 bedtime for a toddler sounds about right.

6. Please send me a reimbursement check for two hundred **thirty-three** dollars.

7. **Ten percent** of insomniacs are also sleepwalkers.

8. For just **five** dollars (**or $5.00 or $5**) more per month, you can have your checks deposited directly into your account.

9. A **$.05** (**or five-cent**) postage increase is set for May.

10. **One-third** of an adult's body is made up of water.

Punctuation, Capitalization, and Writing Numbers Mastery Test Answers

1. I am asking if you would like to rollerblade together tomorrow.

2. Yes, Jean, you were right about that answer.

3. I read in a book, "If all else fails, succeed; if all else succeeds..." (CORRECT)

4. Wherever we go, people recognize us.

5. Whenever Cheryl is in town, she visits her sister.

6. Isabel enjoys the museum although she cannot afford the entrance fee. (CORRECT)

7. It may not be the correct part but I bet that it works. (CORRECT Comma after *part* is optional.)

8. You are my friend; however, I cannot afford to lend you any more money.

9. Paul Simon sang, "I am a rock; I am an island."

10. I asked Ella, "Did he ask for his ring back?"

11. John F. Kennedy Jr. became a magazine publisher and a pilot before his tragic death.

12. Please contact me if you have any questions. (CORRECT)

13. The elections will be held on the first Tuesday of November 2008. (CORRECT)

14. The elections will be held on Tuesday, November 4, 2008, and the polls will be kept open until 8:00 P.M.

15. Carl worried about the hurricane but tried to stay calm and help his family. (CORRECT)

16. I favor green and yellow, and purple is her first choice.

17. I need to locate four states on the map; namely, Minnesota, Michigan, California, and Nevada. (Semicolon after *map* may be a comma.)

18. This is the point that Einstein made: you cannot fix a problem with the problem.

19. Our philosophy teacher thinks that Einstein meant that we cannot stop war by waging war. (CORRECT)

20. A well-made argument was presented for negotiating a peaceful resolution. (CORRECT)

21. The argument for negotiating a peaceful resolution was well made. (CORRECT)

22. A liberally sprinkled dose of humor was very much appreciated. (CORRECT)

23. Our liberal-minded clergyman managed to unite the entire congregation.

24. Our clergyman, who united the entire congregation, was liberal minded.

25. Jan asked, "What did Joe mean when he said, 'I will see you later'?"

26. When I noticed that our dog cut **its** paw, I called the veterinarian right away.

27. Just to be sure, I called three more D.V.M.**s'** offices.

28. "You're right to be concerned," said one veterinarian. "I would like to take a look at your dog."

29. Even though it's 30 miles to the town where that D.V.M.'s office is, I wanted to take the drive. (**OR thirty**)

30. The friendly-looking vet examined our dog's paw and suggested that we have it bandaged.

31. We had pet insurance but still owed $40 in copayment fees. (CORRECT)

32. Our dog was a semi-invalid for a couple of days until she chewed off the bandage. (CORRECT)

33. I guess she did what any self-respecting dog would do by grooming herself.

34. The dog has fully recovered although I will never be the same.

35. I have learned that it's better to be proactive than to have regrets.

36. Wendy thought she knew everything about her mother but found out two years ago that her mother had been married before. (CORRECT)

37. When Wendy asked her mother about this marriage, Ilse (her mother) was hesitant to discuss any details. (CORRECT **OR** use commas instead of parentheses.)

38. "She will go to her grave with some secrets," said Wendy.

39. "Do you understand her need for privacy?" Wendy asked her husband.

40. The wealthy became wealthier during the **1990s**. (CORRECT)

41. The alarm clock went off at **four** o'clock.

42. Many people dread the **15th** of April.

43. The check was written for $13,348.15.

44. The check was written for thirteen thousand, three hundred forty-eight dollars and fifteen cents.